prayer secrets

A Prayer Manual for People of Prayer

MARCUS TANKARD

Copyright © 2015 Marcus Tankard

All rights reserved.

ISBN: 1523382597
ISBN-13: 9781523382590

CONTENTS

1	Prayer Basics	1
2	A Place of Abiding	16
3	Understanding Faith and Prayer	23
4	Prayers to Get Your Needs Met	30
5	Tongues	39
6	Adventures with the Holy Spirit	55
7	Corporate Prayer	70
8	Pastors, Prayers and Regions	86
9	Praise and Worship	101
10	Intercession	109
11	Prayers For Your Government	123
12	Minister's Manna: If You Build It, They Will Come	133
	Meditation Manual	144

1 PRAYER BASICS

Developing a consistent prayer life is the single most important thing a believer can do. You will never arrive at a place of purpose and fulfillment in your life until you learn how to pray according to the principles found in the word of God. The strength of a believer's prayer life is measured by their ability to act on the word and respond to the Spirit. In this study course, we will discuss dynamics of private and corporate prayer.

As we study biblical principles, determine to integrate these truths into your daily living. Knowledge of principles and mechanics doesn't equate answered prayer. We need a spirit of prayer more than a working knowledge of how prayer works. What I share with you during the course of this study is designed to cultivate a spirit of prayer in you. If a person will endeavor to stay under the influence of the following prayer basics, they can be sure of an answer every time.

Prayer Basic #1: Pray From the Position of Faith

Mark 11:22 NKJV
So Jesus answered and said to them, "Have faith in God."

Hebrews 11:1 NKJV
Now faith is the substance of things hoped for, the evidence of things not seen.

Praying from the position of faith is not an option. Jesus gave His disciples a command – "Have faith in God." Faith is how we receive from God. The writer of Hebrews says in chapter eleven, that you can't please God without faith (verse six). Deductive reasoning would suggest then that we have to cultivate a lifestyle of faith if we are going to receive a consistent flow of answers to our prayers.

What is faith? Faith is believing and speaking like the word of God is true. It is the substance or the building blocks of a believer's prayer life. Without faith it is not only impossible to please God, but it is impossible to receive anything from God. You must believe that God is who He says He is and He will do what He says that He will do.

Jesus wouldn't tell you to do something that you didn't have the ability to do. When He says to us, "Have faith in God," its only because we have been given the ability to believe and receive from God. We already have the ability to disagree with what our situations are suggesting and to agree with what God has said. When we bring our hearts into agreement with God's plan for our life, we have taken the first step to praying in faith.

Galatians 5:22
But the fruit of the Spirit is, love, joy, peace, longsuffering, kindness, goodness, faithfulness, gentleness, self-control. Against such there is no law.

When Paul lists the fruit of the Spirit, he places faithfulness, or faith, in the middle of the list. The fruit of the Spirit is the character of God that is produced in us when receive Jesus as our Lord and Savior. From the moment we are born again, we receive the nature of God into our spirits (2 Corinthians 5:17-18; 2 Peter 1:4). When we submit our lives to God, the Holy Spirit produces the character of God in us. One of those characteristics is faith – or the ability to faithfully adhere to what God has said.

You can rejoice that you have already been given faith. The Holy Spirit has been given to you and is helping you to cultivate the God-kind of faith, or the type of faith that God has. What does it mean to have the God-kind of faith? It means to believe, speak, and expect to see what you say come to pass. God exercised this type of faith in the beginning when He spoke and saw the world come into being (Genesis 1; Hebrews 11:2). Now Jesus speaks to us and says "Have faith in God." In the margin of the traditional King James Version of the Bible, the literal Greek text would say, "Have the faith of God," or have God's faith.

Mark 11:22-24
So Jesus answered and said to them, "Have faith in God (or the God kind of faith). For assuredly, I say to you, whoever says to this mountain, 'Be removed and be cast into the sea,' and does not doubt in his heart, but believes that those things he says will be one, he will have whatever he says. Therefore I say to you, whatever things you ask when you pray, believe that you receive them, and you will have them.

When you approach God in prayer, you must pray from the position of faith. This requires that you believe that you have received when you prayed. This means that you have so much confidence in God and His word, that once you have presented the request, you consider problem solved.

1 John 5:14-15
Now this is the confidence that we have in Him, that if we ask anything according to His will, He hears us. And if we know that He hears us, whatever we ask, we know that we have the petitions that we have asked of Him.

Confidence towards God is what produces answers in prayer. If you are not persuaded that God is going to answer your prayers, then why pray? Your time would be better spent quoting a nursery rhyme or wishing on a star. Prayer is not designed to be a wish list. It should be a lifestyle of conversations with a faithful God who is ready to perform on your behalf.

Confidence comes from knowing the will of God. It is impossible to fully receive a blessing that you're not sure he's offering. Before you utter your request, you need to be sure that its something God even wants you to have. The Bible says, "Faith comes by hearing," (Romans 10:17). One minister said it like this: faith begins where the will of God is known.

There was a period of time while I was in Bible school where I struggled financially. While my tuition was paid, I didn't have enough to eat, keep gas in my car, and a host of other expenses that come with living on your own. My parents made it clear that they were not going to be sending me money all the time. In fact when I left school my dad said, "It's time for you to meet God." That meant that he wasn't going to be my source. I was going to have to develop my faith to get my needs met.

The first thing I had to do was find out what the will of God was concerning my material needs. That meant I had to get in the word of God and study it for myself. There's no substitute for studying the word for yourself. Your parents, pastors, or friends can't develop your faith; you have to assume the responsibility for cooperating with the Holy Spirit in the cultivation of your faith.

If faith begins where the will of God is known, then I needed to categorically study financial prosperity. So I went through the Bible and made a short list of scriptures that specifically spoke to my financial situation. I wrote these scriptures down in my journal in different translations and meditated on them. I'm a firm believer that meditation puts you in the verse and it puts the verse in you. As I would read the scriptures I would see myself in the scriptures receiving what was written. I would allow the Holy Spirit to paint a picture in my imagination of these scriptures in my future.

Because there is life in the word (John 6:63), I noticed that as I meditated on the word, my heart began to fully agree with God was saying. This agreement began to form a stronghold in my thinking so that when thoughts of doubt and fear would come, I could answer those thoughts with words of faith. What was happening to me? Faith was being cultivated in my heart as I fed on the Word of God.

When your heart is strong in faith, you are in position to pray. When I began to pray about my financial situation, the first thing that I noticed was my prayer was laced with confidence and not panic. Before when I prayed about the situation, my prayer was more of a complaint or a frantic cry for help. But Jesus never said, "When you pray, be sure it's really an emergency and God will hear you and answer quickly." His instructions were to believe when you pray. Not panic, stress, or worry. Needless to say, that period of financial lack was short lived. God opened a door for me to work for a church both as a Bible school teacher and a musician. That answered prayer opened the door for me to do what I'm doing today, but I would have never entered the doors of that ministry if I'd never entered the arena of faith.

Jesus said, "When you pray, believe that you receive and you will have," (paraphrase). In other words, Jesus was saying, "Trust the process of faith and prayer." Believe that your faith works because you have been given faith of the God kind. And then believe that God is not a liar and that He told you the truth. If God says, "I am your healer," choose to agree with that. If God says, "You can be happily married," then choose to believe that. Determine to believe all the truths of the living word to root out any trace of doubt and unbelief before you pray. Then believe you receive and you will have.

Faith is not something that you just use for your needs in prayer. You must pray from the position of faith in every type of prayer that you pray. Psalms 22:3 says that God inhabits the praises of His people. If that's true, then we need to worship God and expect a manifestation of His presence in our midst. When God comes, His power and ability comes with him. As we bring our faith in worship and praise, we can expect to see God manifest himself on our behalf. He is a rewarder of those who seek him (Hebrews 11:6). The reward of manifestation is reserved for those who believe and seek him.

When you are praying for other people, faith is required. You must identify the will of God concerning the situation that you are praying about; only then will you see the answers that you seek. God never authorized you to pray your will over someone else's life. This is why we must depend on the word and follow the Spirit of God when we intercede for others. God's ways are higher than our ways and His thoughts are higher than our thoughts (Isaiah 55:8-9). Many times we think we know what people need, when in fact we don't have a clue. This is why we must militantly rely on the leadership of the Holy Spirit in prayer and have faith that He will assist us in getting answers.

Prayer Basic #2: Pray From Your Position in Christ

You cannot pray effectively from a false platform of identity. Nothing will deplete your faith and inhibit answers to prayer faster than not having a working knowledge of who you are in Christ. When you received Jesus Christ into your heart everything concerning your identity changed. Now it is your responsibility to spend the rest of your life renewing your mind to the realities of the new identification that you have received.

You should no longer identify with who you were or what you did before Jesus came into your life because you have been born again (John 3:5-6). This is what it means to be born again; you have been given a new beginning. When God looks at you, He doesn't look at you through the eyes of your past. He looks at you through the sacrifice of Jesus Christ. And the blood of Jesus speaks the eternal remission of your sins.

God does not remember any sin that you committed. He sees the righteousness of Jesus Christ and He's able to look at you as if you'd never sinned. But if you are not conscious of the fact that you are forgiven, it will keep you out of the presence of God. When you pray, you must pray from the new identity that you received when you were born again.

2 Corinthians 5:17-18
Therefore, if anyone is in Christ, he is a new creation; old things have passed away; behold all things have become new. Now all things are of God, who has reconciled us to Himself through Jesus Christ, and has given us the ministry of reconciliation.

Most Christians reduce their Christian experience to the forgiveness of sin. But the reality of our salvation far surpasses being forgiven of sin. According to this scripture, when we get saved we become a new creation. One translation says that we become a new species of being. If this is true, then God did more than just forgive you of sin when you accepted Jesus into your heart. The miracle of salvation not only fixes the sin problem, it also fixes the sinner problem.

If God didn't' change the condition of the sinner, it would only be a matter of time before we would all fall back into our old habits and ways of living. In order to safeguard that from happening, God didn't just allow us to say, "I'm sorry," and offer a polite "Ok I forgive you," in return. He wiped out the sin with the blood of Jesus, and gave us a new beginning by making us a new creation from the inside out.

How does God make all things new when a sinner receives Jesus? He not only forgives the sin, but He also removes the sinful nature. "Old things have passed away." That means everything that made you sinful, has been removed. If you were a liar, then the lying nature has been removed. If you were sexual sadist, the sinful nature that promoted that type of behavior has been removed. If you loved to gossip, then God didn't just forgive you for gossiping, He removed the sinful nature in you that allowed you to gossip.

In place of the "old you," God moved in. We know this because it says, "old things have passed away; behold all things have become new. Now all things are of God." When we say, "Jesus lives in me," it's not just a cliché. He really does live in there. This is why the scriptures declare, "Greater is He that lives in you than that is in the world," (1 John 4:4). It's because Jesus is living in your heart.

If Jesus lives in you, then everything He has and everything that He is resides in you as well. Everything that makes Jesus so wonderful and perfect now resides in you and is touching you all the time transforming you into someone that is accepted and pleasing to God. The loving nature that motivated him to die for the sins of the world is now on the inside of you motivating you to pray for the nations.

You have been given joint seating with Jesus Christ. Romans 8:17 says that we are joint heirs with Christ. That means that we have been invited into the company of the God-class to keep company with God the Father, just like Jesus would. God will hear our prayers just as fast as He will hear the prayers of Jesus. We have been raised up to sit together with him in heavenly places and pray out His plan for our lives, our families, the body of Christ and the nations (Ephesians 2). All of this has been done because of the blood of Jesus that changes our identity.

But instead of praying from our position in Christ, many of us pray from a defeated position. When we don't renew our minds (Romans 12:2) to our new position in Christ, we believe the lies that the enemy suggests. Feelings of unworthiness, fear, doubt, and shame bombard our hearts in such a way that we even question whether or not God hears us when we pray. You can stop the flow of enemy's propaganda by reminding yourself of your place in Christ.

Jesus didn't die so you would have a mediocre prayer life. He died so you could pray and get results every time. You should be excelling in your prayer life - not barely getting by with minimal results. Your prayer life should affect your family and your church. The prayers that escape your lips should shake the mountains of influence in any given society – everything from the government to the arts. But your prayers won't go past the roof if you see yourself as a worthless earthworm. Earthworms don't pray "mountain moving prayers," but a believer who knows who they are in Christ can do just that and much more.

1 Corinthians 2:9-10 "Eye has not seen, nor ear heard, nor have entered into the heart of man the things which God has prepared for those who love Him. But God has revealed them to us through His Spirit. For the Spirit searches all things, yes, the deep things of God."

We have heard this scripture for years, but I'm not convinced that it's always been preached in context. Many preachers primarily focus on verse nine where it says, "eye has not seen…ear heard…nor have entered into the heart of man the things which God has prepared for those who love Him." But if you stop right there you miss what God is trying to convey to us. Before we were saved, we were dead in our sin. Our senses were dead to God so we couldn't grasp His plan for our lives. But once we got saved, we became alive to God. Romans 6:11 says, "consider yourselves to be dead to sin, but alive to God in Christ Jesus our Lord." There was a time when I was dead to God; meaning that His plan and His leading didn't pick up on the radar of my heart.

But once I was born again, I became *alive unto God.* That means that my heart has become attentive to what He desires for me. My heart has now become the production center where the Holy Spirit will produce the characteristics of God (which would include the will of God, His thoughts, ways and purposes) in me. This changes the landscape of prayer because it brings me into a whole new arena of praying. Beforehand, I couldn't receive intelligence from the Father. I couldn't discern His plan for my life or prayer assignments for my family and nation. But now my spirit has been custom made to receive from him.

Where my eyes couldn't see, they are open to see clearly. My ears can hear what He desires to say to me concerning my future. I can clearly understand with my heart the comprehensive plans and purposes of God and then pray them out of His heart and into the earth because I have been made able to pray. Yes, I have been made able to pray. When you look at the spiritual make up of my spirit, it is one that is able to keep company with a holy God. I can understand what He announces in my heart by His Spirit. Why is this possible? It's because when I was born again, I was endowed with supernatural abilities and faculties that enable me to keep company with God.

It is from this identity that I pray. I don't pray as one who doesn't know God. I pray as one who is filled with God, can hear from God and flow with God in prayer. God talked to Moses mouth-to-mouth, face-to-face. Oftentimes, we speak highly of the prayer life of Moses, but we fail to realize that Moses wasn't saved. Jesus didn't live in Moses. He wasn't a new creation in Christ. But you are! Because of Jesus, you can experience intimacy with God that surpasses anything Moses had while he was living. God doesn't just talked to you mouth to mouth, He talks to you Spirit to spirit. He does this because He's living in you and touching and inspiring your spirit all the time.

This is the reality of identification that belongs to the believer. We should constantly be reminded of these truths. In the beginning we are thrilled with the truths of righteousness and justification. But with time, we tend to move away from these fundamental truths. However, it is truths like this that convey our identity in Christ and fuel our confidence to stand before God without doubt or a lack of self-worth.

Prayer Basic #3 You Know the Holy Ghost

John 14:16-21
And I will pray the Father, and He will give you another Helper, that He may abide with you forever--he Spirit of truth, whom the world cannot receive, because it neither sees Him nor knows Him; but you know Him, for He dwells with you and will be in you. I will not leave you orphans; I will come to you. A little while longer and the world will see Me no more but you will see Me. Because I live, you will live also. At the that day you will know that I am in My Father, and you in Me and I in you. He who has My commandments and keeps them, it is He who loves Me. And He

who loves Me will be loved by My Father, and I will love him and manifest Myself to him."

The Holy Spirit was given to us to bring the reality of God to us. As much as I love Jesus, he's not in the earth right now. But He said to His disciples, "I will come to you." We see the manifestation of this scripture, in Acts 2 when the Holy Spirit made His entrance in an upper room in Jerusalem. With His entrance came an unlimited possibility of manifestations of the Holy Spirit as authored by Jesus Christ.

John 16:12-15
I still have many things to say to you, but you cannot bear them now. However, when He, the Spirit of truth, has come, He will guide you into all truth; for He will not speak on His own authority, but whatever He hears He will speak; and He will tell you things to come. He will glorify Me, for He will take of what is Mine and declare it to you. All things that the Father has are Mine. Therefore I said that He will take of Mine and declare it to you.

One of the responsibilities of the Holy Spirit is to convey the heart of God to us with accuracy and precision. Jesus said the Holy Spirit would lead and guide us into the fullness of the truth. Truth is defined as the word of God (John 17:17). So the Holy Spirit takes the scriptures and turns them into practical application for our lives - specifically in the arena of prayer. Then, as we need to know, He will show us things to come in the future.

God never intended for believers to take cues in prayer from the news media. God wants us to be in a flow of continual dialogue with the Holy Spirit, so He can transmit prayer assignments to us daily. As we respond to His leading in prayer, we can know the news before it happens. We can have an effect on events concerning our families, cities and nations by following the Spirit in prayer.

This is what I call praying supernaturally. It is the most exhilarating thing I have experienced next to leading someone to Jesus Christ. Once you get a taste of praying supernaturally, you will never resort to lifeless prayer formulas and rituals. When you go on an adventure with the Holy Spirit and He gives you words to speak out in prayer, it fills a void in your heart that cried out for the supernatural.

Some people wonder how is it possible to pray with this type of power. It is not a mystery when we know how the Holy Spirit leads. Recognizing His leading is the first step to following Him in prayer. Jesus boldly declared in John 14:17 that "you know Him (the Holy Spirit), for he dwells with you and will be in you." Many believers struggle to follow the Spirit because they don't realize that they already know him. They may not be aware of how well they are acquainted with Him, but searching the scriptures will reveal to us the workings of the Spirit all around us. If we can connect the dots between His activities, it will develop a discerning heart in us to follow him in every area of our lives – specifically in our prayer lives.

John 16:7-8
Nevertheless I tell you the truth. It is to your advantage that I go away; for if I do not go away, the Helper will not come to you; but if I depart, I will send Him to you. And when He has come, He will convict the world of sin, and of righteousness, and of judgment.

Before we ever accepted Jesus Christ as our Lord and Savior, the Holy Spirit was wooing us to get saved. He was the one convicting us of sin and convincing us of the lordship of Christ. This is one of the most important jobs of the Holy Spirit because conviction is pivotal to people getting saved.

John 3:5-6
Jesus answered, "Most assuredly I say to you, unless one is born of water and the Spirit, he cannot enter the kingdom of God. That which is born of the flesh is flesh, and that which is born of the Spirit is spirit."

2 Corinthians 5:17-18
Therefore if anyone is in Christ, he is a new creation; old things have passed away; behold, all things have become new. Now all things are of God, who has reconciled us to Himself through Jesus Christ, and has given us the ministry of reconciliation...

The Holy Spirit not only convicts us of sin, He is the one who makes the new birth possible. When you are born again, old things are passed away and all things become new. That means that everything that you were leaves and everything that God is comes in you. This is the greatest miracle you will ever experienced because it translates you out of the kingdom of darkness and put you into the kingdom of God.

The only way the born again experience is possible is by the Holy Spirit. Jesus makes it plain, "That which is born of flesh is flesh, and that which is born of the Spirit is spirit." The Holy Spirit is the power of God in operation for our salvation. So before we were saved, the Holy Spirit was convicting us of sin. Then once we make a decision to make Jesus our savior, the Holy Spirit comes in and enables us to be born again. But that's not all the Holy Spirit does. He is an expert teacher.

1 John 2:27
But the anointing (the Holy Spirit) which you have received from Him abides in you, and you do not need that anyone teach you; but as the same anointing teaches you concerning all things, and is true, and is not a lie, and just as it has taught you, you will abide in Him.

The Holy Spirit desires to teach you all things. Everything that concerns you is a concern to him. So it is His desire to bring truths out of the word to you that are applicable to every situation that presents itself. The vocabulary of the

Spirit is the word of God. He's called the Spirit of Truth, or the truth-giving Spirit. That means that He will bring truth to your spirit by way of the scriptures that you study.

Sometimes when I read the word, I find myself getting "stuck" on a particular passage. I can keep reading in the chapter or go to another book of the Bible altogether, but somewhere in my heart, that scripture that I was "stuck" on is still rolling around. That's the Holy Spirit shining His light on the scriptures. The reason He is illuminating that scripture to me is because there are things that He wants to say to me. There is a revelation that will bring me into a greater flow of profit and progress found in the scripture. I can choose to ignore it (because I'm too busy to study or the scripture makes me feel uncomfortable). But it would be to my benefit to acknowledge and respond to the life coming out of that scripture. The life that I'm speaking of is the Holy Spirit endeavoring to lead me into all truth.

Many believers experience the same thing but they don't realize that it is the Holy Spirit's ministry in operation. We are looking for the Holy Spirit to come in and flow like a mighty wind with lightening and thunder. But that's not the way Jesus said the Holy Spirit would come to us. There may be times when the Holy Spirit moves in a spectacular way. But the best way to be led by the Holy Spirit is to be led by what the word says. The Bible says that He will lead us into all truth, or the word of God. The gifts and manifestations of the Spirit are available to us, but we won't recognize when the Holy Spirit wants to move if we don't recognize him speaking to us out of the word.

Acts 2:4
And they were all filled with the Holy Spirit and began to speak with other tongues, as the Spirit gave them utterance.

Another area that the Holy Spirit is found working is in our prayer life, specifically speaking in tongues. This is a very basic truth that must be embraced if we are going to participate with him in prayer. When we are filled with the Spirit, the Holy Spirit gives us utterance in an unknown tongue. Speaking in tongues is a prayer miracle made possible by the Holy Spirit. We will discuss this in detail in another lesson, but for now its important to note that the Holy Spirit brings a supernatural language to our spirit. We hear these syllables on the inside and allow them to escape our lips.

This is what we call speaking in tongues. Paul says that when we speak in an unknown tongue, we are speaking mysteries. The mystery that we are speaking is God's perfect will over the situation. The Holy Spirit draws on the intelligence of God concerning the situation, and then conveys that to us in an unknown tongue. The Holy Spirit begins supplying this supernatural utterance to our spirit the moment we are filled with him. We begin to engage in hearing and obeying him at that very moment.

This intimate exchange with the Holy Spirit takes place from the inside out. As a believer, you can't be any closer to the Holy Spirit than you are right now because He is in you. When you acknowledge that He is in you, it makes it easier for you to follow him and pray with him.

You know the Holy Spirit better than you think you do:

1. He convicted you of sin.
2. He made it possible for you to be born again.
3. He teaches you the word.
4. He enables you to speak in tongues.

If you can see the places in your life where He has been active, it will awaken your ability to follow him in prayer. The Holy Spirit has infinite knowledge of any situation you want to pray about. He is ready to lead you and bring you into greater productivity in prayer. Sometimes when we talk about following the Holy Spirit in prayer, many believers move prayer into the realm of impossibility. Don't allow yourself to feel disqualified to pray supernaturally. The supernatural realm belongs to you. Jesus died so you could experience His presence. You do that by allowing the Holy Spirit to bring you into His presence.

Being led by the Spirit isn't hard when you realize that you already know him. Be confident in this. Recognize and respond to him and you'll see a greater flow of power to get results in prayer.

Prayer Basic #4 Keep the Word First

Hebrews 2:1
Therefore we must give the more earnest heed to the things we have heard, lest we drift away.

This is probably the most important dynamic to prayer. The word of God is our guide and vocabulary in prayer. Jesus said that the Holy Spirit would bring His words back to our remembrance. But this only happens when we have stocked the shelves of our heart with His sayings.

God says that His ways are higher than our ways and His thoughts are higher than our thoughts. It is hard to have a productive conversation with anyone who doesn't share the same paradigm or frame of reference. God solves this problem by putting His thoughts in a book: the Bible. Then He gives us specific instructions to search this book diligently and digest the truths in it (Joshua 1:8; Isaiah 34:16).

A regular diet of the word will produce a renewed mind. Romans 12:2 says to be transformed by renewing your mind. The word of God is the launching pad for your destiny. When you choose to read, study, and meditate on the word of God, you accelerate your spiritual growth and expand your potential. The word of God has the ability to expand your capacity to receive from God because it brings you into the knowledge of promises that you haven't received yet. When you embrace these truths, you can exercise your faith to receive their manifestation.

Another way to describe renewing your mind is to bring yourself into agreement with God. Romans 8:7 says that the carnal mind is hostile towards God. When you are hostile or uninviting towards the ways of God, you can't receive the things of the Spirit. Remember, the measuring stick for successful prayer is your ability to act on the word and follow the Holy Spirit. The word brings your mind into agreement with God's ways and thoughts so you can freely receive what the Spirit of God has to offer you. You will never move into a consistent flow of the Spirit in prayer until you bring your mind into agreement with the word of God.

A renewed mind is the foundation for the move of the Holy Spirit. The word of God dismantles unnecessary traditions, false doctrines, and inhibitions to the move of the Spirit. When your mind is in agreement with God, your capacity is expanded to receive, recognize, and respond to promptings of the Spirit. So it is very important that you be intentional about renewing your mind. It takes effort to maintain a regular diet of the word, but the reward of answered prayer makes it all worth it.

I love how the word keeps me balanced in prayer. When you develop a lifestyle of prayer and you make corporate prayer a priority, it's easy to pick up what I call doctrinal baggage along the way. Doctrinal baggage includes beliefs or spiritual habits that were God breathed and God inspired for one period of time or specific prayer assignment, but quickly became a lifeless tradition later on.

For instance, some of the prayers that are read in some of the mainline denomination churches (Methodists or Presbyterians) are beautiful. If you ever get an opportunity to read and meditate on some of these prayers, it will greatly enrich your life. These prayers were powerful at the moment of their inception. But men have made them a "prayer monument" and rather than receive present day inspired prayers from the Spirit, they simply rehearse what He inspired years ago. They do this so much so that they read these prayers regularly at the expense of a new expression the Spirit in prayer. That may have been what the spirit was calling for years ago, but what is the prayer the Spirit is calling for today?

I remember there was a time when we would dim the lights at our church during our corporate prayer meetings. Initially when did this to help people focus on God and move their attention off themselves and other people. It was to help people "tune into" God. But soon, this practice became doctrinal baggage because it became frowned upon if someone turned the lights on. Praying in the dark doesn't make God answer your prayer any sooner than praying with the lights on.

Anything you do in prayer becomes doctrinal baggage when you place it on the same level as the written word of God. When you allow something that God inspired you to do in prayer to become a law that cannot be challenged by the word and the Spirit, you've got a problem. Sometimes we can be guilty of what Jesus said when He addressed the Pharisees (Luke 7:9; 13): "All too well you reject the commandment of God, that you may keep your tradition…making the word of God of no effect…"

One of the things I loved about the ministry of Kenneth E. Hagin was his dedication to teaching on prayer with simplicity. Jesus instructed him to teach by precept and example. So if you attended a day service with Brother Hagin, he would teach the word with simplicity and then demonstrate prayer by inviting you to pray with him for the nation. It was in sessions like this that all the doctrinal baggage and non-essential traditions were shaved off and balance was returned to the prayer lives of the people present. The word of God can rescue you from wrong thinking in prayer, but you must submit your mind to it regularly.

Matthew 4:4
But He answered and said, "It is written, 'Man shall not live by bread alone, but by every word that proceeds from the mouth of God."

I love to pray. I wish that I could say that I equally loved to read the word of God. But that would be less than truthful. I'm sure I'm not alone in my struggle to read the word consistently. One thing that helped me change my perspective was this scripture. Jesus said that we were to live by every word that proceeds out of the mouth of God. In other words, God's word is fuel to our prayer time. It provides the sustenance necessary for me to move quickly and efficiently in prayer

I used to find myself getting bored with the word. I would complain within myself because the word didn't seem to excite or thrill me. But after meditating on this scripture, I could see that the word of God was not designed to thrill me every time I read it, but it will nourish and provide fuel for me and my prayers. The word of God is to my prayer life what gas is to my car. I never complain about how I have to put the same kind of gas in my car every week. Because I realize my car requires fuel, I don't hesitate to take the time and spend the money to put the proper fuel in my car.

We have to exercise the same diligence with the word, whether we are thrilled or not. The desire to be thrilled comes from an unhealthy appetite for entertainment. When we aren't entertained by a particular TV show, we just turn it off. That attitude tries to creep into our relationship with God and we find ourselves turning off from necessary spiritual disciples. We cannot allow that kind of thinking. The word of God is the supply that God designed to nourish our spirits and bring fresh vigor and vision to our prayer lives. To neglect the word is to shut off the flow of answers in prayer.

There are a series of topics that I would suggest that people of prayer be very well versed on in order to stay balanced in their praying. Probably the most important thing to study is how to walk in love. Jesus said that when you stand praying, forgive (Mark 11:25-26). It is so easy to allow pride to come in when you are getting answers to prayer. We can think more highly of our selves than we should only to find that we began isolating ourselves from people that we don't think know as much as we do. That's not the life that God authored for us to experience. We are to be vitally connected to him and to the other believers (John 15).

One of the first indications that you are getting off balance in prayer is that you feel the need to separate yourself from other believers – specifically the local church. The word of God says don't forsake the assembling together with your church (Hebrews 10:25). So for you to do that is direct disobedience to the word. No matter how much we grow, we are never exempt from obeying the written word of God. But when we allow pride to poison our minds, we allow foolish thinking and exempts from something as simple as coming to church and having a good attitude. Study and memorize scriptures on love because the more pure your love walk, the more powerful your prayer life (1 Corinthians 13).

Another topic that you should study on a regular basis is who you are in Christ. We've covered this topic briefly in this lesson book, but you should study it extensively in your private devotion. I encourage you to take a colored pencil or highlighter and underscore verses in the new testament that bring attention to who you are in Christ. Scriptures that have phrases like *in him, through him, by him, in Christ, because of Christ,* etc., will give you a clearer picture of God did in Christ for you. Jesus didn't just forgive you of your sin. What happened to Jesus in His death, burial and resurrection changed the whole landscape of prayer for the believer. We need to be conscious of this revelation as we pray.

After we have experienced a season of answered prayer, it's easy to analyze how or what we prayed and reduced answered prayer to a formula or method. Being aware of who you are in Christ keeps you doctrinally centered on the finished work of the cross and not the finished work of your praying. God doesn't answer prayer because you got all the syllables right. God answers prayer because Jesus washed you in the blood, gave you access to the presence of God, gave you a new identity and spiritual make up so you could hear God, and He filled you with His Spirit so you could know, experience and work with him in prayer. Its not your slick praying that makes power available. It's the finished work of the cross that authorizes and empowers your prayers. Never forget that.

Review Questions

1. What is faith?
2. Why is it important to know God's will?
3. What does it mean to pray supernaturally?
4. How do you stay balanced in your prayer life?

Tweetable Moments

- Faith is believing and speaking like the word of God is true. @MarcusTankard #PrayerSecrets
- Jesus didn't die so you could have a mediocre prayer life. @MarcusTankard #Prayer Secrets
- Confidence comes from knowing the will of God @MarcusTankard #PrayerSecrets
- The Word of God is our guide and vocabulary in prayer. @MarcusTankard #PrayerSecrets
- The Holy Spirit was given to us to bring the reality of God to us. @MarcusTankard #PrayerSecrets

2 A PLACE OF ABIDING

John 15:7
If you abide in Me, and my words abide in you, you will ask what you desire and it will be done for you.

Prayer is easy when you can identify God's will for the situation. I learned a long time ago that it's better to agree with God than to try and change His mind. Prayer is not about getting "your way" all the time. It's about bringing your heart into perfect union with him so that out of that agreement you can pray His plan.

Jesus tells us in John's gospel, if you will abide in him and allow His word to abide in you, you can ask and receive. That sounds like a blank check if you focus on the last part of the scripture. But we can't forget there is a condition in the beginning: abide in me and my words abide in you. What does it mean to abide in him?

When I think of abiding in him, I think of a bird and their nest. Generally, when birds want to lay eggs, they make a nest. The nest is the place of reproduction. They abide in the nest on and off until the eggs hatch and the baby chicks can fend for themselves. As a Christian, abiding in Christ is like a bird abiding in the nest. If you want to be productive in prayer, then you must abide in Him by continually returning to your place of prayer. To abide in him is to abide in His word and follow His Spirit.

Abiding in the Word

Jesus said if you will allow His words to abide in you, you have mastered half of the battle for effective praying. God only answers prayers that originate with him. I want you to think about that for a few seconds. God will only answer prayers that originate with Him. You may be thinking, "I thought the scripture said that I could ask whatever I want and I would have it." Prayer is a little more complex than just spouting off our wants to God. Remember, he's not Santa Claus. There is an "ebb and flow" to getting answered prayer but we have to dispel the myths surrounding the subject before we can walk in the truth.

When you allow the word of God to abide in you, it will change the way you think, talk, and act, but most of all it will change the way that you pray. God desires that you renew your mind with His word to the place that when you make a request in prayer, its really not you asking - it's Him asking. This simply means that now once you agree with His will and His plan to the extent that you desire it for yourself, he's ready to give to you.

1 John 5:14
This is the confidence that we have in him. That if we ask anything according

to His will, he hears us and if he hears us we have the answer to our petition.

God is not deaf. It's not that God can't hear your prayers. It could be that your prayers are not in line with His will for your life. God's plan our lives exceeds our highest expectation. He knows what will not only make us happy today, but what will make us happy for eternity. We can be so shortsighted that we ask and accept mediocre relationships, jobs and opportunities. God can see the end from the beginning and desires to culture our praying in a way that we pray eternally minded and not "right now" minded.

When I identify the will of God for my situation, then I can pray it back to God knowing that He will hear me and answer my prayer. So that means sometimes we have to pray before we pray. What do I mean by that? Sometimes we have to pray and get in the word of God to find out what God's will is for a particular situation before we can pray about it. Until we know the will of God on a certain matter, we can't pray for definitive results. Praying for what we perceive to be the will of God can get us into deep trouble and long-term disappointment. The first step to answered prayer is to get in the word and His presence and find out what God's will is on any given matter. Once you have His will, God can have His way.

Search the Word Diligently

Before you endeavor to ask God for anything, you should make it your aim to find out what God has already said about the situation. The first way that you do that is to get into the word of God.

Proverbs 3:6
In all your ways acknowledge Him, and He shall direct your paths.

When you search for the will of God in His word, you are acknowledging him. Reading and meditating on scriptures is how we renew our mind and move into a place of agreement with God. For example, if you are in need of healing, you should read scriptures on healing. This will eradicate any wrong thinking concerning God's will on healing. Once you take on God's thoughts concerning healing as your own, you are ready to pray and receive His will. Until you have identified God's will, you are playing "guess and check" with God in prayer. This isn't the confidence that John talked about. The confidence that we need for answered prayer is found in knowing the will of God.

Testimonies vs. Word

Commit to being a student of the word. This will safeguard you from living on testimonies. While testimonies are encouraging and inspiring to our faith, they don't feed our faith. Only the word of God will do that. Jesus said that you live and thrive on the words that proceed out of the mouth of God. That tells me that yesterday's revelation of the scriptures is not enough to sustain you or your prayer life. You must identify what God is saying to you right now out of the word. It's called the rhema word. It's what God is highlighting concerning your situation.

Never base your praying or prayer patterns on past testimonies or the experiences of other believers. Many people have taken the experiences of other people and turned them into "prayer doctrines." They've endeavored to duplicate the same exercises in prayer and it's been disastrous because they didn't get the same results as the other person.

One intercessor tells the story of how they would go out into the woods and lay in a log for hours and pray during the winters. He would pray so long that the snow would melt. There's nothing wrong with this man praying in a log until snow melts. The problem comes in when someone who lives in south Florida tries to mimic the same thing and it doesn't snow in that part of the country. This is an extreme example, but I pray you understand the point. Don't make any one else's experience your measuring stick. Be inspired by their stories, but at the end of the day, you must stick with the Word.

When a person follows the Spirit to pray a certain way, that's not your cue to copy or mimic them in any way. The leading that they received came out of a revelation from the Holy Spirit instructing them. If you try to do the same thing without having the same revelation and leading, there is no life in it to produce the results you are seeking. It's like a husband merely trying to copy another guy's method to impress his wife.

Doing something not produced from relationship and intimacy with the Holy Spirit will always diminish results in prayer and any other area for that matter. Keep it biblical and original. If you are inspired by a testimony and you sense the Lord leading you to do something similar, then fine. But don't allow anyone else's prayer life to be your measuring stick. Stick with the word and follow the Holy Spirit in your own heart.

Abiding in God

Jesus said if you abide in me and my words abide you. Abiding in the Word means to allow the Bible to align your thinking with God's will. Hebrews 4:12 says that the Word of God is alive. If the Word is alive and the Word is abiding in you, then the Word should be constantly changing you. This change takes place as you become more acquainted with God's will for your life. What does it mean for you to abide in him?

Abiding in Christ goes beyond reading the Word. You can read the Word apart from Him and come up with something in your mind that He didn't say. God desires to lead you and guide you into the fullness of the truth and into a greater reality of destiny. But you can't do that just by searching the scriptures. The word of God is a big part of it, but John 6:63 says that we can search the scriptures looking for life, and not realize that the scriptures are leading to a person, Jesus. If we are not careful, we can become so mechanical and analytical with the Word it drives us from His presence. We endeavor to intellectually walk by faith instead of being led by the author and the finisher of our faith, Jesus Christ.

We must be careful that we worship the God of the Word and not the Word of God. God's Word is not merely a law that we live by. God's Word is the expression of His mind and His will. It is through the Bible that we can identify His plan for the church, the nations and humanity in general. But there are specific details concerning our personal lives that aren't outlined in the word. We can know that its God's will for us to own a home or get married, but the specific home we are to buy or the person we are to marry is not listed in Bible. These are things that the Word of God will condition our heart to receive directly from God. But we will never come into the knowledge of these details if we exalt the Word above the God and the reality of His presence.

Abiding in God means that our relationship with Him goes beyond just a mere acquaintance with His word. When we abide in Him, it means that we have a continual flow of communication with God. Just because you have a relationship with someone doesn't mean that you are enjoying the fruit of satisfying fellowship with him or her. The currency of any relationship is communication. But if there is no communication, the relationship is weak and has no foundation to build upon. When you have regular fellowship with God it builds strong faith and builds fortitude in you to do great things for God.

Fellowshipping with God

Exodus 33:7-11
Moses took his tent and pitched it outside the camp, far from he camp, and called it the tabernacle of meeting. And it came to pass that everyone who sought the Lord went out to the tabernacle of meeting which was outside the camp. So it was, whenever Moses went out to the tabernacle, that all the people rose, and each man stood at his tent door and watched Moses until he had gone into the tabernacle. And it came to pass, when Moses entered the tabernacle, that the pillar of cloud descended and stood at the door of the tabernacle, and the Lord talked with Moses. All the people saw the pillar of cloud standing at the tabernacle door, and all the people rose and worshipped, each man in his tent door. So the Lord spoke to Moses face to face, as a man speaks to his friend. And he would return to the camp, but his servant Joshua the son of Nun, a young man, did not depart from the tabernacle.

Joshua was so hungry for the presence of God that even after the "prayer service" was over, he remained there to pray. This is the type of tenacity that breeds confidence to take cities and lands. In God's presence, there is a transmission of Himself that you receive. The residue of that presence remains and enables you to do things that you wouldn't normally do. Joshua believed that he was well able to take the city of Jericho because he knew the God who was giving him the instructions. By spending time in God's presence, you develop an intimate acquaintance with Him that births boldness to do His will. This is a pronounced difference from what the other spies were saying. Their self-esteem wouldn't allow them to enter into the land God had already promised them.

Because Joshua had spent time in the presence of God beholding His glory, he was changed into another man - a man fit to take the land. When you abide in God's presence like this, your acquaintance with Him changes you. Things that used to inhibit you or make you fearful melt away as you increase in the knowledge of the one who lives in you.

Paul's Ministry

Philippians 3:10
That I may know Him and the power of His resurrection, and the fellowship of His sufferings, being conformed to His death,

2 Timothy 1:12
For this reason, I also suffer these things; nevertheless I am not ashamed, for I know whom I have believed and am persuaded that He is able to keep what I have committed to Him until that Day.

Many times we wonder what's the secret to success in ministry. It isn't a secret - it's right here in the Bible. Paul had a very close relationship with God. He didn't just know about God; he knew God. This is how Paul was able to go into regions where he knew the religious people would hate him and still preach the gospel. There is a continual flow of power into your life when you maintain a consistent prayer life. This power produces boldness that will outrun your inhibitions concerning the will of God.

Your prayer time should be the launching pad for your destiny. When you spend time with God, you can download from His heart concerning His plan for your marriage, family, businesses, ministry and whatever else concerns you. The river of God's presence that you experience in prayer will lead you into the fullness of His plan for your life, but you have to step into the river first. You do that by abiding in God. You don't just come into His presence periodically. If you are serious about the plan of God and want to do mighty exploits for God, you have to be intentional about getting into His presence daily.

Some of us know prayer principles, but we don't know God. We have prayer formulas and prayer manuals, but we really don't know God. There is an intimacy that comes from experiencing His presence for yourself. You can have all the scriptures and the formulas for prayer, but without an intimate knowledge of God, your prayers will lack the depth and power to move heaven.

If you want to get results in prayer, you can't just run to God when you need something. It's like asking a favor of a stranger. Desire to know Him, not just receive from Him. When you actually know Him, receiving from Him isn't an issue. The intimacy fuels your faith and enables you to stand firm. God never designed prayer to be a time where you dish out all your wants and complaints while He strategizes on how to fix your life. Prayer is fellowshipping with God over His plan for your life. When you and Him can come to a place of agreement in these areas answered prayer will be the flow of your life.

Cultivating the Spirit of Prayer

Many of us have read lots of books out there on prayer, and have memorized the formulas. The problem with prayer formulas is that we tend to approach God like a machine. We tend to punch spiritual buttons and hope God will act the way we want. But there must be a desire to know in whom we have believed.

God's power doesn't flow because we memorize the Word. Real faith comes from knowing the person behind the scriptures. Paul never said, "I know what formulas and gimmicks I have believed and worked." No, Paul knew God. And the way he knew God is the same way that you will know God: fellowship. Faith in the Word and fellowship with God are inseparable because it is fellowship that breathes life into your faith. When your desire to know Him causes you to pray, His presence accommodates you and strengthens you to do great exploits. Then and only then will we be truly persuaded of the promises of God and be able to pray in faith.

One of the best ways to cultivate the spirit of prayer is ask God to make you hungry. Everyday I say, "Lord, cause me to always pray." I never assume that just because prayer is exciting to me today that it will always be exciting. God helps me to stay hungry for prayer by revealing Himself to me in His word and His presence. When He reveals himself to me in new and exciting ways it woos me further into His presence. The more I experience Him, the more I desire Him. The more I desire Him, the more I seek Him.

Sometimes our prayer life becomes robotic because we forget that we are talking to a person. God is a divine person. So when you are making a request, praying in tongues, or even reading the bible, you are enjoying an audience with him. Don't allow yourself to reduce these things to mere spiritual disciplines for a religious person. This is how we fellowship with God and experience the reality of His personality.

Another way to cultivate the spirit of prayer is by getting around people who pray. This is why we have prayer schools, prayer clinics, and minister in prayer conferences. It is because events like that foster a community of praying people who can encourage one another. Different people carry different parts of the anointing. When you assemble with them and you all can pray together, the part of the anointing that you carry to pray can be strengthened.

The old adage that says, "You are who you hang around," is most certainly true. You partake of what you fellowship with. So get around people of prayer. If you are struggling in your prayer life, attend some corporate prayer meetings. It may initially feel uncomfortable, but hang in there. You didn't learn how to ride a bike or how to swim the first time. Keep working at it and you will be better at it. Prayer is easy, but it is not without effort.

Review Questions

1. What does it mean to abide in the word?
2. What was Paul's secret to success?
3. What is prayer?

Tweetable Moments

- Reading and meditating on the scriptures is how we renew our minds. @MarcusTankard #PrayerSecrets
- Prayer is fellowshipping with God over His plan for your life. @MarcusTankard #Prayer Secrets
- Your prayer time should be the launching pad for your destiny. @MarcusTankard #PrayerSecrets

3 UNDERSTANDING FAITH AND PRAYER

John 15:7
If you abide in Me, and my words abide in you, you will ask what you desire and it will be done for you.

Jesus makes it clear in this passage of scripture that faith and prayers are inseparable. God is pleased when we believe His Word to the extent that we renew our minds with it and converse with him about it. God's thoughts are not our thoughts, but He put His thoughts in His Word. When we take God's Word into our minds we are taking on God's thoughts. This makes us able to have intelligent conversation with Him concerning His plan and His ways.

What does that have to do with faith? Everything! Romans 10:17 says faith comes by hearing the Word of God. When you read the Word, you not only discover God's plan for your life, you also build confidence in God and His plan for your life. The confidence that you gain from reading God's word translates into the faith you take into prayer. And it's this faith and confidence that pleases God and releases His power towards you.

Mark 11:23 KJV
whosoever shall say unto this mountain be thou removed and be thou cast into the sea and shall not doubt in his heart but shall believe that those things which he saith shall come to pass he shall have whatsoever he saith.

Faith is not discriminatory. This scripture starts off by saying whosoever shall say unto this mountain. This means that faith and prayer will work for anybody. It doesn't matter if you've been saved thirty years or thirty days, faith in God will see you all the way through to the end. No matter what your ethnic background, income bracket, or religious affiliation. Faith in God will see you through. We must learn the mechanics of faith and how to apply them to our relationship with God and our individual destinies.

Faith will work for whosoever and it will work on whatsoever. It doesn't matter how long that problem has been present in your life - faith will move it. You don't have to be intimidated by the presence of a problem. I have a saying, "If a problem enters the ring of my life, my faith can eat it." My faith is up to the test! Why can I say that? Its because my confidence is in God and not in my self or my ability to make something happen. My dependency is on God's ability and not my own. Faith and prayer will work on relationships, healing in your physical body, finances, career, ministry or any other area that you can think of. Faith will work if you'll learn how to work.

How Does Faith Work

Faith comes by hearing, but faith doesn't work by hearing. Faith works by speaking. Sometimes we think if we can read enough faith books, listen to enough sermons on faith, attend enough faith conferences and listen to enough faith preachers we will have great faith and do mighty faith exploits. But that's not how the walk of faith works.

Mark 11:24 KJV
Therefore I say unto you, what things soever ye desire, when ye pray, believe that ye receive them, and ye shall have them.

When I teach on the subject of faith, I generally ask the question "how many times do you see the word say or saith in this scripture?" Say or saith is in this passage three times. Then I follow up with another question: "how many times do you see the word, believe?" Believe is in this verse one time. Without playing word games or semantics I want to suggest to you that the emphasis in this scripture is speaking.

Jesus says that you can uproot any problem in your life with your speaking. I want you to focus on the crux of Jesus' discourse on faith. Your faith filled words can uproot any mountain in your life. Mountains of debt, depression, fear, torment, cancer, or loneliness can be removed and cast into the sea of your past by the faith filled words that escape your own lips.

The key is speaking the word of God. Someone may say, "Pastor Marcus I believe that." But my question is do you believe enough to speak it? Demons believe the Word, but it's not working for them. And the Word will never work for you if you don't believe and speak.

Romans 10:9-10 KJV
That if thou shalt confess with thy mouth the Lord Jesus and believe in your heart that God has raised him from the dead, thou shalt be saved. For with the heart man believes unto righteousness and with the mouth confession is made unto salvation.

This is one of the primary scriptures that we use when preaching the gospel. When we pray what we call the *sinner's prayer*, we confess with our mouths the lordship of Jesus Christ because of what we believe in our heart to be true: that God raised Jesus from the dead. In verse ten, we can see why the sinner's prayer works. With your heart you believe unto righteousness, but with your mouth confession is made unto salvation.

What does that mean? Your believing changes the condition of your heart, but your confession changes the situation. Salvation is unlocked by the confession of your mouth. Jesus said that your mouth speaks from the abundance of your heart. So from a place of abundant faith, you speak what you believe to be true concerning Jesus Christ and His sacrifice. In response to your faith, you are translated out of the kingdom of darkness and translated into the kingdom of light.

This is the essence of salvation. You believe with your heart, confess with your mouth what you have believed and then you receive salvation. Notice that you believe with your heart, but you don't receive with your heart. Your heart is responsible for producing faith and it does that when the word is sowed. Your heart has the capacity for faith. You heart has the capacity to believe God and His promises. But that potential is not released until the word is sowed. Once the word is sown into your heart, there is a supernatural force produced called faith. Faith is ability to believe what God has said to the extent that you think, speak and act like He told you the truth.

But just because you have faith doesn't mean that you have released your faith. The moment you release your faith, you are ready to receive. How do you release your faith? You release your faith by speaking. I like to say it this way: you believe with your heart, but you receive with your mouth.

When you get saved, you believe in your heart unto righteousness. In your heart you believe that the penalty for sin is death and gift of eternal life is found in Jesus Christ. Then you take it a step further and speak what you believe. Once you speak what you have believed concerning the lordship of Jesus Christ, you receive salvation. This is what it means when the scripture says that you confess unto salvation.

Faith comes by hearing but it doesn't work by hearing. Faith works by speaking. Remember Jesus said that you have to speak to the mountain. This means that believing is not enough. Faith moves mountains, but it won't move anything until it moves you. And the first part of you it will move is your mouth. Hearing the word has the potential to change your believing, but it's your speaking that changes what you are seeing.

Saying and Praying

Jesus focused on the "speaking" aspect of faith. So it is important to note that faith is released by words. When you speak the word you release your faith. This is our first opportunity to act on God's word. Faith-filled confession expresses our agreement with what God has said and it is our agreement with Him that engages His power into our prayers.

When we talk about speaking the Word, it's important that we cover both aspects of speaking: saying and praying. Confessing the word encompasses both. You're confessing the Word when you talk about the goodness of the Lord with other people. You're confessing the Word when you talk to yourself or read the scriptures out loud while meditating. But you are also confessing the Word when you pray. Faith is released when words are spoken no matter the context of the speaking.

Jesus said, "Whosoever shall say unto

this mountain…" So you can speak to the mountain. When Jesus talks about mountains, he's using a mountain as a symbol of the problems in our lives. You can speak directly to the problem. Jesus said so. He said speak to the mountain. There are some problems that you don't have to talk to God about. Just use your authority and speak to it. Death and life is in the power of your tongue.

God spoke "Let there be light," and there was light. Jesus spoke to the storm and said, "Peace, be still." Jesus has distributed the same authority to you. Sometimes we've been talking to God about the mountain so long that we think God should move the mountain. Other times we've talked to other people about the mountain. But talking to God and other people about the mountain is not the same thing as talking to the mountain. Sooner or later you've got to target your faith and speak directly to the mountain. Speak to the debt. Speak to the sickness. Speak to the confusion. Speak to the situation at work. You have to speak to it.

As a general rule, I don't pray about things I should be speaking to. I determine what I should be speaking to or praying about based on what scriptures I can find. If I can find a scripture that promises me something, I don't have to pray about it. If God has already given it to me, then I don't need to pray about it because God isn't the one keeping it from me. Once God gives you something, the only thing that keeps you from receiving it is the devil or your wrong thinking.

For example, I never have to pray about healing. I can pray about it, but I don't have to. The Bible says in 1Peter 2:24 as well as Isaiah 53, that "by His stripes we were healed." When Jesus bore my sin, He also took on sickness and disease. Every stripe that He took on His back is to be a reminder of the provision that He made for my healing. Healing is a done deal.

So I don't have to ask God to heal me. He settled my healing over two thousand years ago. So if I'm going to say anything to anybody, it's going to be to the devil first. I say to the devil, "Take your hands off my body right now. I command every lying symptom to get out of this body in Jesus name." Then I speak to my body and say, "Body you line up with the Word of God. Every disease and every virus that touches this body dies instantly. I speak to every cell, organ and every tissue of my body and command it to function in the perfection to which you were created to function." That's how you speak to the mountain of sickness and disease.

If you are going to pray about healing, your prayer needs to be concerning how to practically walk it out. Your prayer should be for wisdom and counsel concerning what doctors to visit, what medications to take, and how to maintain your healing. But there's really no need to ask God for something He's already given you. Use your authority to get the devil off of you so you can receive the fullness of God. That's not something you have to pray about per se, it's just something you need to do by speaking directly to the mountain.

What if you have a financial need? God has made provision for financial and material needs. Remember, if you can find scripture that indicates God has already given it to you, then its best to use your faith saying to the mountain versus praying about the mountain. Second Peter 1:3 says that God has given unto us all things that pertain unto life and godliness. Psalms 23:1 declares the Lord is my shepherd so I don't have to be in want. That means I don't have to want for food, water, shelter, wisdom, counsel, opportunity or money. Second Corinthians 9:8 says that Jesus was made poor so that we might be rich.

All of these scriptures convey that God has already taken care of our financial and material needs. There's nothing else for him to do. God is not the one keeping the money and opportunities from us. The devil is doing that. He tries to steal, kill and destroy everything that concerns us. But God has given us authority to speak to the mountain and to speak to the devil.

You can speak directly to debt and say, "Be removed from my life in Jesus name. I call you paid in Jesus name. I speak to the money and I say come to me in Jesus name. I speak to the opportunities and say come to me in Jesus name." Just saying that out loud conditions your heart to recognize and receive the opportunities when they come your way. All of this happens without you praying about it. Your saying can activate your deliverance.

Don't Be Legalistic

I'm not advocating being legalistic about confessing the Word versus praying the Word. It is important to remember that faith works by saying and praying. Jesus said to speak to the mountain. But in the same sermon He also said, "Therefore whatsoever things you desire when you pray, believe you receive them and you shall have them." So it is perfectly ok to pray about those things that you desire. However, even if you pray about it, you will still have to speak in line with what you pray. You can't pray in faith about something, but then talk doubt and fear when you go throughout the rest of your day. Even if you pray in faith, you have to also speak in faith.

What I'm advocating for is a greater expression of faith in God and His Word. When you speak the Word over things that God has already given you authority over, you are acting like the Word of God is true. Acting like the Word is true is how we please God. Lets find the ebb and flow of the life of faith where we can pray in faith, speak in faith and then receive the end of our faith.

This is the difference between using our authority and being skillful with our authority. We should always endeavor to take the highest route in prayer. What is the highest route? You can quickly identify this by asking a series of questions: What does the Word say? What has Jesus provided for me in redemption? Why have I not already received my answer? Is the answer to my request something God has to give me or something I need to receive?

I have run into similar situations with people desiring the baptism of the Holy Spirit. People come to services seeking the baptism and praying, "God, please give me the Holy Spirit." But after the outpouring in Acts 2, you never find people asking for the Holy Spirit.

In fact when believers were ministering to people who weren't filled with the Spirit, they asked, "Did you receive the Holy Spirit when you believed?" (Acts 19:2). Notice that they didn't ask, "Did God give you the Holy Spirit?" The Holy Spirit had already been given. The question was (and still is): have you received.

The Holy Spirit is a gift that you receive. The same can be said of healing, prosperity, and wisdom. This is why it is so important that you spend time in the Word of God identifying what God has provided for you in Christ. When you are aware of these realities, you can benefit from them and use your authority to keep the devil from stealing them.

Release Your Faith

Mark 11:24
What things you desire when you pray believe that you receive them and you shall have them.

Matthew 21:22
And all things, what things you desire in prayer, believing you shall receive them.

The most important thing is that you release your faith when you speak to the mountain and when you pray. Since faith comes from the Word, you need to have a lush supply of God's Word in you concerning the request that you are making. Until you get scriptures in your heart about the issue, you don't know what God has to say about it. Before you make a request you need to make sure it is God's will for you to have what you desire.

Don't just pray. Know what you believe when you pray. If you pray without knowing what the Bible says, then you're not praying – you are wishing. God never told us to wish. Our instructions are to abide in Him and allow His Word to abide in us. Then we can ask and receive answers to our prayers.

You can't release your faith until you know what you believe. One minister had a prayer line for people who wanted him to agree in prayer with them. Most of the people that were in line had prayer requests but they didn't have scriptures that indicated what they believed concerning the requests.

Before you can ask God about finances, healing, or marriage, you've got to be well versed about what He has already said concerning. Find out what God is saying and then line your saying and praying up with that. Then and only then will your prayers be answered.

5 TONGUES

People have asked the question, "Why do you talk about speaking in tongues so much?" It's not that I talk about speaking in tongues a lot, but I think people tend to have a lot of questions about it so there's a lot of discussion surrounding it.

Speaking in tongues is distinctive of the dispensation of grace that we live in and enjoy today. We don't see anyone speaking in tongues in the Garden of Eden. None of the judges of Israel spoke in tongues. The prophets experienced the demonstration of God's power in exponential proportions, but they never spoke in tongues. Kings and military leaders experienced the power of God to conquer nations and rule wisely, but none of them ever spoke in tongues.

All of the gifts of the Spirit listed in 1 Corinthians chapter 12 have their entrance in the Old Testament. Miracles, signs and wonders marked the ministry of Moses from its inception. Elijah and Elisha saw the physical world affected by the anointing that resided in a mantle they wore. Joshua saw the elements of the universe align themselves to accommodate the will of God in battle as the "sun stood still." The prophets saw the unseen realm open to them where angels, apocalyptic visions, and even the similitude of God was discerned. But none of these spoke in tongues.

Its so interesting to me that God would reserve this supernatural demonstration for the church age. Out of all the ways that He chose to make His entrance into the New Testament church, why would He choose speaking in tongues? Surely God didn't save the worst or the least manifestation for last. Why would God choose to infuse all the manifestations of the Old Testament into a seemingly ornamental act of speaking in tongues? I believe that it's possibly more to it than just bumping gums and getting cotton mouth. If we can identify the purpose and power of speaking in tongues, I believe we can unlock the power of God to not only change our prayer but to also change our world.

Speaking in tongues is not a mystical practice that an elite number of Christians experience. Neither is it something that is merely ornamental to the life of a believer. It is a supernatural experience in prayer where an individual can pray without being limited by intellect. When you speak in tongues, you are speaking a supernatural language from the Spirit of God that is God's perfect will concerning the situation up for discussion. And we know from previous chapters that if we pray anything according to His will He hears us. If He hears us, we have the answer to our petition.

Filled With the Spirit

Acts 2:1-4
When the Day of Pentecost had fully come, they were all with one accord in one place. And suddenly there came a sound form heaven, as of a rushing mighty wind, and it filled the whole house where they were sitting. Then there appeared to them divided tongues, as of fire, and one sat upon each of them. And they were all filled with the Holy Spirit and began to speak with other tongues, as the Spirit gave them utterance.

This was a monumental day for the church. After days of praying and seeking God concerning the next series of steps for them and the global church, this group of believers experienced an outpouring of the power of God that proved to change the world forever. This outpouring was the first time that the baptism of the Holy Spirit and speaking of tongues was experienced.

One of the things that I must point out is that the Holy Spirit doesn't speak in tongues. Verse four is very clear on who was speaking. They spoke *as the Spirit them utterance.* Tongues are indeed the language of the Spirit, but it is a language that escapes our lips by our own permission and volition. This scripture does not say that the Holy Spirit overpowered anyone. Although church culture may have promoted a desire in us for an uncontrollable experience, this is not what happened in this scripture.

It says that they were all filled with the Holy Spirit and from that *filled* state, the Holy Spirit gave them something to say. We know that they heard what the Spirit said because they spoke it out. So if there is a formula or method to speaking in tongues, its found right here in this scripture.

First they were filled with the Spirit. Being full of the presence of the Holy Spirit will always precede speaking in tongues. And there is no secret as to how to be filled with the Spirit. In Luke 11:13, Jesus said, "If you then, being evil, know how to give good gifts to your children, how much more will your heavenly Father give the Holy Spirit to those who ask Him!" The disciples were praying when the Holy Spirit was poured out in Acts chapter 2. This tells us that simply asking God to fill you with the Holy Spirit is one way to experience the baptism of the Holy Spirit.

Although you can simply ask and receive the Holy Spirit, there are a lot of people who will not receive that way. Some people won't release their faith until someone lays their hands on them. That is perfectly okay because God has made provision for that with the ministry of the laying on of hands. There are three instances in the book of Acts where people received the baptism of the Spirit through the laying on of hands (Acts 8:14-17, 9:17-18 and Acts 19:6).

Being filled with the Spirit is the prerequisite to speaking in tongues. What must be stressed here is that speaking in tongues is a supernatural expression. When you speak in tongues, you're not speaking "jibber jabber," or merely making up a language as you go. This language is inspired by the Holy Spirit (of whom you must be full of).

Supernatural Language

And they were all filled with the Holy Spirit and began to speak with other tongues, as the Spirit gave them utterance. Acts 2:4

There is no room for error in this scripture if you will accept what is written without adding any further interpretation. It says that they (the people who were gathered in the upper room) were all filled with the Spirit and began to speak with other tongues. Who began to speak with other tongues? All of the people in the upper room who were filled with the Holy Spirit.

The miracle in this scripture is not found in who is doing the speaking. We know that the people who were filled with the Spirit did the speaking. The miracle is in the language being supplied to the speakers. This language is not something that was premeditated or learned. It is a language that goes beyond the ability of the mind to construct. It is the language of the Spirit designed to convey the mind of God in a way that guarantees answered prayer.

When you speak in other tongues, you are speaking from a place that your mind cannot find. That is because the language doesn't come from your intellect; it comes out of your spirit where the Holy Spirit lives. Job 32:8 say, "there is a spirit in man and the breath of the Almighty gives him understanding." Your spirit is the catcher's mitt for the Holy Spirit.

When the Spirit of God wants to convey the supernatural language of tongues, He's going to bring that language to your spirit, your heart. I use these terms interchangeably because they locate where God lives in you by the Holy Spirit. God doesn't live in your brain or your foot. He lives in the center of your being; the part of you that is eternal, your spirit. So it is no mystery why when the Holy Spirit wants to feed you intelligence that He brings it from the place where He lives – your heart.

So when you are filled with the Spirit and you want to speak in other tongues, you don't need to look any farther than your own heart. Why? Because the giver of the utterance is in you and He is going to feed your heart utterance that is to escape your lips. The scripture said that they began to speak in tongues as the Spirit gave them (their hearts) the utterance. That means the Spirit gave them the words to say, but it was up to them to speak.

The Holy Spirit is not going to make you speak in tongues anymore than He is going to make you speak English or whatever your native language. He will prompt, inspire, encourage and nudge you to speak. But under no circumstances is He going to reach His hand down your throat, grab your tongue and make you speak in an unknown tongue. To expect the Holy Spirit to do that is to give Him a job that doesn't belong to Him. Remember: you are the one who speaks. His only function in this instance is to provide you with what to say. That may not be as spectacular as we would like but its no less supernatural than what God designed.

My wife and I often minister the baptism of the Holy Spirit in our church services. We lay hands on people to receive the fullness of the Spirit and many times the power of God fills them so much that they fall down to the floor. But many people (that even fall to the floor) don't speak in tongues immediately. So I've asked them, "When I laid hands on you did you feel the power of God?" They all have replied, "Yes." My next question to them is, "Did you have a desire to say anything that wasn't in your known language? In your imagination can you see yourself speaking in tongues?" Again they answer, "Yes." So then I ask them, "Well why didn't you speak out what you were hearing in your heart? Why didn't you allow yourself to speak what you felt like speaking?" And without fail, they say something like, "I didn't want it to be *me* speaking. I wanted to make sure it was really the Holy Ghost."

But to expect the Holy Spirit to speak in tongues is contrary New Testament doctrine. The Holy Spirit doesn't speak in tongues – you do. I understanding the line of thinking that says, "I don't want to fabricate an experience with the Holy Spirit that isn't legitimate." I understand that feeling all too well. But we have to make sure that we are clear on what our role is and what the Holy Spirit's role is not. Remember: the Holy Spirit's only job is to supply you with utterance. He doesn't take charge of your tongue and cheek muscles in order for you to speak in tongues. You take control of your physical body and you speak out what He is saying to your heart. This is how you speak in tongues.

They All Spoke in Tongues

Notice that the scripture didn't say, "they were all filled with the Spirit and some of them began to speak in tongues, but others started to sing songs and get real happy." No, everybody who was filled with the Spirit began to speak in other tongues. Maybe some of them sang or got real happy. But one thing is for sure: all of them were filled and all of them spoke in tongues.

Some have erroneously assumed that everyone who is filled with the Spirit doesn't speak in tongues. I like to say it this way: everyone who is filled with the Spirit has the ability to speak in tongues. Whether or not they actually speak is up to them and their faith. According to the scriptures, everyone who was filled with Holy Spirit in the book of Acts spoke in tongues – no exceptions.

It is important to note that you don't

have to speak in tongues to go to heaven. The gift of the Holy Spirit is a gift. I like to call Him the gift that keeps on giving because the Holy Spirit brings with Him a multitude of expressions and ministries that are a "gift" to our lives, families and destinies. The ministry of the Spirit is not required to get you into heaven; the blood of Jesus secured eternal redemption for you. The Holy Spirit's ministry to us is designed to be an assistance to our walk with God and to our calling to good works here on earth. Jesus said that we needed the ministry of the Holy Spirit. So it would be a good idea for us to embrace Him and His entire ministry to us and through us. But should we decide to not admit His gift into our lives, it doesn't put our salvation in jeopardy.

God's Swiss Army Knife

I like to view speaking in tongues as a Swiss Army Knife. The term *Swiss Army knife* generally refers to a pocket Knife with a sharp blade and a myriad of tools (screwdriver, can opener, etc.). The benefits of speaking in tongues go beyond prayer. This spiritual language has an ability to produce constructive, spiritual growth in you as you speak. This happens in many different ways. We must learn to utilize all the benefits of speaking in tongues if we are going to reach our full potential in prayer.

One of the fastest ways that we can increase our awareness of these benefits is by studying the Word of God on the subject. Speaking in tongues can unlock operations of the Spirit for our lives, families, churches and nations. But we must find out what the Word of God has to say on the subject so we can attach our faith to it. When you know that God has given a tool to you, you can utilize it for your success. But you can't profit from something if you are not aware that it even exists.

Praying for the Unknown

Romans 8:26
Likewise the Spirit also helps in our weaknesses. For we do not know what we should pray for as we ought, but the Spirit himself makes intercession with groanings which cannot be uttered.

Jesus called the Holy Spirit a helper (John 14:26). It is therefore the nature of the Holy Spirit to help us in any arena of life – prayer included. When the Holy Spirit made His entrance into the church, the believers spoke in other tongues as he, the Holy Spirit, gave them utterance. It is important to remember that the Holy Spirit didn't do the speaking. The believers were the speakers; the Holy Spirit simply provided utterance.

The Holy Spirit comes to our aid in prayer by alleviating one of the greatest weaknesses: ignorance. Notice the scripture says that there are times we don't know *what* we should pray for." It's not that we don't know *how* to pray. We have the best prayer manual on earth – the Bible. So we know how to biblically pray and get answers. The problem comes in when you have the formula for answered prayer, but you don't know what the will of God is for the situation. Until you can identify God's plan for any given situation, you can't pray in faith about it.

Have you ever encountered a problem where you knew you should pray, but you didn't know how or what to pray about it? Have you ever had a problem that seemed to be so complicated you didn't even know where to start in prayer? When your mind is flooded with confusion or the will of God concerning a relationship or a financial issue is not clear, you can't just pray and confess a set of scriptures, walk away and hope something comes out.

For example, maybe you are having trouble with one of your children. You've talked to your spouse about the problem and you couldn't seem to come up with anything. You've read books and even went to workshops, but nothing is working. You know that it's God's will that you live harmoniously with your child. In fact you may have scriptures that you confess over your children daily. All these things are good, but the Holy Spirit was given to help us make up the difference where our efforts fall short. You don't have to play guess and check with your family relationships when you have the Holy Spirit. Engage heaven's supply in this relationship and you'll see a change! How do you do that? By prayer and supplication in the Spirit.

Put some extra time aside (maybe while driving or doing laundry) and pray for your child. This time when you pray, pour your heart out to the Lord about them. Tell the Lord everything that you've done thus far concerning the relationship. Express to Him why this is so important to you. Let the Lord know that you are not accusing him of not doing anything. You just want to engage His help on this matter. Then pray in tongues.

So many times we walk away from prayer before the Holy Spirit has had an opportunity to assist us with supernatural utterance. We figure that we've done our part by praying the scriptures. But that's not all of it. Remember, the Holy Spirit doesn't do the praying for you; He helps you to pray by giving you supernatural utterance. You must actively give the Holy Spirit an opportunity to assist you in prayer by submitting your mouth to Him and praying in tongues.

As you are praying, the Holy Spirit is giving you the perfect prayer to pray concerning your child. When you receive utterance from the Spirit in prayer, it is the perfect will of God concerning the situation. He's not going to inspire you to pray anything that God doesn't want. Why? Because the Holy Spirit knows what the mind of God is. When the Holy Spirit is giving you utterance to pray, He's drawing on the limitless wisdom of God. Jesus said the Holy Spirit would draw on what He has and knows for you and distribute it to you. One of the ways that the Holy Spirit does this is in prayer.

When you pour your heart out to God, pray the scriptures that you know are His will in the situation, and then begin to pray in tongues about the situation, you have fully engaged the assistance of God on your situation. Don't stop praying too soon. Sometimes we stop praying after we have talked to God about the problem. But if you stop there, you've probably spent most of the time complaining about the problem. Some of us stop after we've prayed the scriptures that we know. But no matter how much scripture you know, your knowledge of the situation is still limited. You may think you know what's needed in the situation but only God knows what is really needed.

There is a specific victory that God has in store for your situation. There are a million and one ways that God can deliver you out of trouble. You don't need a million ways to get out of trouble – you just need one. Praying in tongues brings laser sharp accuracy to your praying that identifies the specific way God wants to lead you into victory.

Mysteries and Secrets

1 Corinthians 14:2
For he who speaks in a tongue does not speak to men but to God, for no one understands him; however, in the spirit he speaks mysteries.

The first time I read this scripture, I was in high school. At that time my friends were deciding what they would do after high school graduation. Some were going to the army; others were going to this college or that university. A lot of people were going to stay in our city and get a full time job. As the school year progressed, the pressure was on me to make a decision concerning what I would do after graduation. The problem was I didn't have a clue what I wanted to do.

The only thing I was sure of, was God had called me to preach. I'd seen myself preaching the gospel, praying for the sick, teaching and training ministers and all sorts of other things in the ministry. In fact, a few times, God spoke to me in very spectacular ways with concrete confirmations from other people concerning things I would do in the ministry. So whether or not I was going to be in ministry was never a question. I needed to know what the next series of steps were for my life and ministry.

One day I was listening to a pastor by the name of Charles Cowan. He was preaching a sermon on speaking in tongues. That night he read this scripture in 1 Corinthians. Pastor Cowan read verse two and defined what the word *mysteries* really meant in this passage. It literally means hidden truths or secrets.

At that moment, something like a bomb went off in my heart. I knew that was a key to me understanding what God wanted me to do. God knew what I was supposed to do after high school, but that was still a mystery to me. I found out that when I pray in tongues, I am speaking out hidden truths and secrets. Psalms 25:14 says that the secrets of the Lord are with those who reverently fear him. God will reveal the secrets regarding your future. But you must reverence Him enough to ask Him and not try to do it by yourself.

I decided to go on a 21day fast. I didn't eat meat, sweets, drink sodas, or watch TV for three weeks. Fasting has an ability to refocus our affections so we can hear from God accurately. When you add prayer with fasting, you condition your heart to receive what God wants to say. That's exactly what my life required at the time. I didn't want to waste time and money in the wrong school or career when God had a perfect plan for my life.

During those three weeks, I determined to pray in tongues more than I had my entire life. Some days I would pray in tongues for an hour at a time. Instead of driving straight home from work, I would go to the church and walk around the property and just pray in tongues. Those were precious moments with God where He downloaded things into my spirit that I'm doing today.

At the end of those three weeks, I had so much more clarity concerning the will of God for my life that I could strategize and make a plan for my post graduation life. God spoke to me about moving to Tennessee to live with my dad and help him plant their first church in Murfreesboro. I'm so glad that I obeyed him because that church plant launched me into the next phase of my life, which included moving to Tulsa, Oklahoma and going to Bible school.

The decisions that you need to make for the next phase of your life don't have to terrify you. Fear of the unknown doesn't have to paralyze you. We have been given divine help. The Holy Spirit was given to us so we can navigate through the plan of God with speed and accuracy. Don't allow the devil to imprison you with ignorance and confusion. The answers concerning the next series of steps for your life are closer than your next breath. The Holy Spirit is living in you right now and He's ready to give you utterance in an unknown tongue concerning your future.

Praise and Worship

1 Corinthians 14:14, 17 For if I pray in a tongue, my spirit prays, but my understanding is unfruitful… For you indeed give thanks well, but the other is not edified.

When you worship the Lord in other tongues, your flesh is put to the side and your spirit is released to be free to express itself in full abandonment to God's presence. When we worship in our native tongue, we are limited to the songs that we've learned, or the vocabulary that we possess to express our love and adoration for God the Father. But when you begin to speak and sing in other tongues, there is something released out of your spirit that not only changes you but also changes the atmosphere.

Psalms 22:3 states "God inhabits the

praises of His people." In other words, we can experience a greater awareness of His manifested presence when we welcome Him with praise and worship. And when God inhabits our praise, He doesn't just come and sit down. He comes with the purpose of engaging with everyone that is present and ready to receive.

One night I was at church praying about my future. As my prayer time was coming to a close, I just began to worship the Lord. I can remember walking down up and down the aisles of the church worshipping the Lord. As I walked down the middle aisle toward the front of the church, I turned to my right and I fell into a trance. In a moment I was seeing a vision of the church full of people worshipping the Lord. I looked towards the platform and there was a full band with singers worshipping with the most beautiful music I'd ever heard. When I looked on the faces of the people, there was a glistening glow coming from their faces as they worshipped. Many times I struggle to find words to describe what I saw.

I looked towards the back of the church and the doors opened. As I waited to see who would walk in, I saw Jesus walk through the door. At that moment, the tangible manifested presence of God increased exponentially. I struggled to stand. He walked in the sanctuary and I noticed that he began to walk up and down aisles and rows as I had been doing earlier. He began to minister to different people and they were healed instantly. It was the most amazing thing to witness. Jesus walked down the middle aisle and as he got up to the front of the church where I was standing, he stopped and looked directly at me. He said, "I desire to manifest myself in worship services and meet the needs of my people. But the atmosphere must be in order for me to move. I will move in an atmosphere of praise and worship."

The Bible says that God seeks those who will worship him in spirit and in truth (John 4:24). God is not after an intellectual exercise set to music. He wants worship to flow from the very core of our being. But many of us are so saturated with emotional junk that it's hard to relate to God beyond our intellect. We try to calculate everything from the length of worship, the words and lyrics of worship and where we worship. God says, "Put all the extra stuff away and just stick to worship in spirit and in truth."

What does worship in spirit and truth mean? Well first it means that true worship comes from a place your mind can't find: your spirit. True worship isn't predicated on what God has done for you or what He's promised you. True worship springs from an awareness of the holiness of God and His worthiness of all worship and all glory. Your mind can't wrap itself around the eternal faculties of God. So there is only so much that you can't expect from your mind in the area of worship. God says dig down into the deepest part of you and worship. The deepest part of you is your spirit. Allow your spirit to have expression in worship. How do we do that?

Paul told us to sing psalms, hymns and spiritual songs (Ephesians 5:18-20; Colossians 3:16). Psalms are poems and odes. I like to think of them as love letters. These things are to commemorate the goodness of God and turn our attention from outward problems and put our eyes on His goodness and faithfulness. Hymns are simply songs. When most people think of hymns, they think of old songs from a dusty book. But hymns have nothing to do with whether a song is old or modern. A hymn is simple a song set to music. There are songs birthed from the Spirit of God that can help convey the depth of your heart to the Lord in worship. Use that to your advantage.

There is lot of great music available to us for worship. Be careful to make sure that what you are worshipping with is actually worship. A lot of what is called worship is not worship at all. It's just a prayer set to music. There's nothing wrong with that, but when its time to worship, lets not make a request; lets worship. Sometimes we have a difficult time worshipping with songs that have nothing to do with us. But true worship is not about us; it's about Him.

Then Paul says to worship with spiritual songs. What are spiritual songs? They are songs that originate from your spirit. This would include singing in tongues and prophetic songs. In 1 Corinthians 14:15, Paul says, "I will sing with the spirit, and I will sing with the understanding also." Singing with your spirit is singing in other tongues. As you sing in tongues, worship springs out of you that transcends a song that you learned. It goes beyond the latest trending worship song. This worship is not predicated on the song choice for the worship service. The Holy Spirit inspires this worship.

Building Yourself

Jude 20
But you, beloved, building yourselves up on your most holy faith, praying in the Holy Spirit…

I looked up the word *building* and it simply means to construct by putting parts or materials together or in position (relating to time, place and order). When you pray in tongues, you are building something. You're not just making sounds and noises. There is something supernatural that is taking place. Prayer is supernatural! Not just because of the effect of answered prayer. The prayer that you pray itself is supernatural. That prayer is an instrument in the hand of God to build.

Jude says that you can build yourself up by praying in the Spirit. This means that I can take responsibility for my own building. Building can be a metaphor for your spiritual development, a business, a ministry, relationships or whatever it is that you are in need of at the time. You can build it by speaking in other tongues. It's time that we learn how to be skillful with the things of the

Spirit so we can build internally and externally.

I remember there was a time when God was leading me to do something with my career outside of my comfort zone. Before this I'd been a vocational pastor and traveling minister. But God was calling my wife and I to move into some other arenas entrepreneurially. Whenever God begins to shift you, your family, or your career, it requires another level of consecration. You'll find out real quick how submitted you are to God when a shift requires radical obedience.

If we were to obey God in this area, we would run the risk of being ridiculed. At that time my circle of friends and colleagues frowned on bi-vocational ministers. The belief was if God had called you to preach, then your calling should be able to fund you and your family. While I do believe the same thing, I also believe that the leading of the Spirit trumps everyone's opinion (including yours). I think the main fear for me was that if I started the businesses, I wouldn't have time for ministry. I wanted to continue traveling and ministering on a consistent basis so I felt like running businesses would hinder that.

And then there were insecurities about whether or not I had the business savvy to even be an entrepreneur. Most of my immediate family have multiple streams of income from their businesses. I've always been the odd family member who didn't have any businesses and did ministry full time. I never really thought I had what it took to start a business and do it well.

So there were all these fears and insecurities flooding my mind in the midst of the voice of God rolling around my spirit about this business. I had to make a decision to yield to God and build obedience in my spirit. So guess what I did? I started praying in the Spirit. There is a scripture in Hebrews that says, "I have come – in the volume of the book it is written of me – to do your will, O God." I would take that scripture and pray it everyday (sometimes multiple times throughout the day) and then pray in tongues. As I prayed I would allow my mind to paint a picture of what my unbridled obedience would be like when I started the business. As I prayed I began to set my affections on this business by faith. I say that I did it *by faith* because in the natural, my emotions were giving me fits about it.

The more I prayed about this business in other tongues the stronger I became in my spirit. What was happening? I was constructing something in my spirit. The gifts, talents, abilities and opportunities necessary to start a successful business were being built in my spirit as I was praying. When I began to build internally, I prepared my heart and body to build externally. Today, in addition to being in full time ministry, we have four successful businesses. Psalms 127:1 says, "Unless the Lord builds the house, they labor in vain who build it." But when you allow God to build in you and through you, your success in life is imminent.

This will work for your relationships as well. You may have trouble being kind and patient with a loved one. There may be a particular person who has hurt you over and over again, and you can't seem to stop keeping a record of what was done wrong to you. If you will pray in tongues about it, Jude 20 and 21 says that you can keep yourself in the love of God. What does that mean? That means that you can build an operation of love in you that will outrun the bitterness the devil is trying to fortify in you. You don't have to allow all sorts of strife and hate become a stronghold in your life. What is coming against you is not greater than what can come out of you. If you will meditate on love scriptures as you pray in tongues, you can build a solid love walk in your spirit. And from that place of love will flow witty and innovative acts of love that can override the offense that's trying to overtake you.

Maybe you're having trouble talking too much. Too many words can sabotage even the closest relationships. You can build temperance into your spirit by praying in the Holy Spirit. Praying in the Holy Spirit will teach you how to discern the leading of the Spirit on your words. Remember, as you pray in tongues, the Holy Spirit is giving you utterance. You can sense His presence on those words as you release them. Give your attention to the sensations that you feel as speak those words.

Then allow that to develop discernment in you of when God is telling you to speak and when He wants you to be quiet. When you're talking to people throughout the day and you sense the presence of the Holy Spirit lift off your words, that's your cue to back off. Tactfully and respectfully be quiet and take introspect of what you're saying and what you shouldn't say. This type of discernment can safeguard your relationships from unnecessary offense. Take the responsibility for your success in life and build what your calling requires into your spirit.

Self-Improvement

1 Corinthians 14:4
He who speaks in a tongue edifies himself, but he who prophesies edifies the church.

Another way to describe the edification that takes place when you speak in tongues is self-improvement. God has so much in store for all of us. He's said in Jeremiah 29:11 that he has good plans for us. Many of you reading this book have prophecies that you've received that haven't manifested yet. I believe that a large part of the lack of manifestation is that God is preparing you for what He's prepared for you.

God knows if you're ready to receive the answer to your prayer or the manifestation of a prophetic word. He knows the condition of your character and your integrity. So one of the first things that happens when you begin praying in the Holy Spirit consistently, is that your conscience is awakened. God wants you to become aware of things in your life that may inhibit your progress or sabotage your success. Remember, God is on your side. And He doesn't want you to have a prophecy manifest and then your race is over. God wants you to get into the ebb and flow of success.

Sometimes we can be "event-minded" concerning the plan of God. Your walk with God is not as simple as cause and effect. There is a flow to your success in God's plan for your life. You have to find that flow and stay in it. The way you do that is by allowing your heart to be conditioned to doing things God's way. Speaking in tongues does just that. As your conscience awakens to what the next level requires, you can begin making adjustments immediately and make steps in the direction of your promise and prophecy.

For instance, God may have given you a word that you will be debt free. Some of us would wait until God magically paid our debts off. But if we did that, we'd probably be waiting a long time. God is not beyond miraculous debt cancellation. But if you don't allow God to change you (debtor), then after God brings you out of debt, you'll find yourself right back in debt again in a few years. You've got to find the ebb and flow of a debt free life. The first step to doing that is allowing God to awaken your conscience to the destructive financial habits that created the debt in the first place.

Praying in other tongues will awaken you to things you need to change financially, but also the good habits that need to be reinforced and increased. God will talk to you about your finances as you pray in the tongues, and He won't bring fear or condemnation with it. The Lord will teach you to prosper. But you must show up to class; prayer is the classroom. Allow Him to condition your heart to the flow of success that he's designed for you.

I have preached this message to singles many times. You don't have to wait for the ideal candidates to present themselves to you. You can build the image of a happy and healthy marriage in your spirit while you're waiting. In doing so, you prepare yourself to be the ideal spouse and you condition your heart to the leading of the Spirit so you will recognize a good spouse when they present themselves.

I know this from experience. When I went to Bible school, I just knew for sure that I would find a mate. But after two years of school and one year of full time ministry, I wasn't married and there weren't any prospects in sight. One day I ran across a scripture in Hebrews that helped target and release my faith more accurately.

Hebrews 11:3
By faith we understand that the worlds were framed by the word of God, so that the things which are seen were not made of things which are visible.

God created the world with His words. Jesus said that we could create and frame things with our words as well (Mark 11:23). So I decided to get in the

Word and identify the type of woman God wanted me to marry. Genesis says that Eve was suitable and complimentary to Adam. So I placed that in a prayer confession for my wife. I would say every day, "Father I thank you that my wife is suitable and complimentary to the call of God on my life. I declare that she is beautiful, anointed and intellectually stimulating." And then I would begin to pray in the Holy Spirit.

As I prayed in tongues, my conscience awakened to the things that were hindering me from being the ideal spouse. Things like laziness, rudeness, lust and a host of other things that I had lurking around that I wasn't conscious of. As God made me aware of these things, I exposed every one of them to the Word of God. This enabled me to bring them into the obedience of Christ. What am I doing? I'm building a healthy marriage in me before I ask for a woman's hand in marriage.

While I'm working on myself, my confession is working externally. As God's Word shaped the universe, my words are going out to many fronts shaping, framing and rearranging events and people to accommodate a place of meeting for my wife and I. A desire to leave my current position at a church in Tulsa grew immensely during this time. I began to seek out counsel from other ministers on how to get into world missions. So after a lot of praying and researching, I left my job and moved to Alabama to begin building a strong missions ministry.

One month after I moved to Alabama, I met my wife at the church of the man who became our pastor, married us, ordained us, and dedicated our baby. God has a plan for your life! If you will pray it out, He will infuse you with ability internally and opportunity externally to accommodate the manifestation of His plan. You don't have to wait on God to initiate what I'm talking about. He has already stated that He has a plan for your life. Initiate your own progress in the plan of God by praying it out. You start that by simply confessing what you know to be true about the plan praying in other tongues consistently.

The Gateway to the Supernatural

Kenneth E. Hagin said, "Praying in tongues is the gateway to the supernatural." I heard him say this on more than one occasion. And like a parrot I repeated it without completely understanding the meaning behind the statement. Speaking in tongues is not a mystical thing. Its not like you speak in tongues and all of the sudden there is an explosive expression of power. It may look like that's what happens, but there's more to it than that.

It's not enough to know what is happening as we pray in the Spirit, we need to press in to understand why and how the supernatural is released so we can be more intentional and cooperative with the Spirit when we pray. I can lend my faith more to praying in other tongues when I'm aware of what is happening as I pray.

We know that the Holy Spirit is responsible for the born again experience because Jesus said that we are born of water and the Spirit (John 3:5-6). But when he filled the church, the first expression of him that we see is speaking tongues. Speaking in tongues is the ministry of the Holy Spirit, the helper. I sincerely believe that when we learn to embrace His initial ministry to us, we will be led into greater expressions of His ministry of help.

Acts 2:4 AMP
And they were all filled [that is, diffused throughout their being] with the Holy Spirit and began to speak in other tongues (different languages), as the Spirit was giving them the ability to speak out [clearly and appropriately.

When the Holy Spirit fell on the believers in Acts chapter 2, he began to give them utterance and they spoke out what they were hearing. The formula was real simple: hear and obey. Hear what the Spirit is saying and respond to that by speaking out what you hear. The consistent hearing and responding in prayer is designed to develop your acquaintance with the Holy Spirit's voice. The more familiar you are with His voice, the less likely you are going to be deceived by the voice of a stranger.

Hearing and obeying is crux of our walk with God. That's all He really asks us to do: hear His word, believe His word and obey His word. We can develop our ability to hear the Holy Spirit by speaking in tongues. Every time you speak in tongues, you have to listen in your heart for the utterance that only He can give and then respond to what you hear by speaking it out of your mouth. Every utterance in tongues is an encounter with the Holy Spirit that develops your discernment in spiritual things.

Hebrews 5:14
But solid food belongs to those who are of full age, that is, those who by reason of use have their senses exercised to discern both good and evil.

The writer of Hebrews says that your spiritual senses learn to discern good and evil one way: by using them, or by practice. In other words, the way you develop in the things of the Spirit is by flowing in the things of the Spirit. The more you interact with the Holy Spirit in prayer, the more he can lead you into other operations and manifestations. God is ready to take you on an adventure in prayer. But you won't travel far with Him if you don't know how to follow Him. Speaking in tongues is the beginning of that following. If you can follow Him as He inspires you to speak in an unknown tongue, you'll be able to recognize when He's inspiring you to pray or prophesy in your known tongue.

Remember that the same Holy Spirit who convicted you of your sin, is the same Holy Spirit who enabled you to be born again. The same Holy Spirit that speaks to you in the Word of God is the same Holy Spirit that is inspiring you to speak in tongues. The Holy Spirit is not a set of triplets. It's the same person inspiring you in each of these areas. The goal is to make the connection between all these activities of the Spirit. Doing so will develop an awareness of him that can be followed in prayer and every other area of your life.

1 Corinthians 12:7
There are diversities of gifts, but the same Spirit. There are differences of ministries, but the same Lord. And there are diversities of activities, but it is the same God who works all in all. But the manifestation of the Spirit is given to each one for the profit of all.

The manifestation of spiritual gifts is the supernatural flow of the Spirit Kenneth E. Hagin was speaking of. When you pray in tongues, you become aware of the moving of the Spirit in ways that you would not have been conscious of had you not been praying. There are so many different flows of the Spirit in prayer and outside of prayer. When you develop the gift of speaking in tongues, you have entered a new realm of prayer where the possibilities are endless.

Review Questions

1. What is speaking in tongues?
2. How do you speak in tongues?
3. What are biblical ways to receive?
4. Why is speaking in tongues the gateway to the supernatural?

Tweetable Moments

- 🐦 The disciples were praying when the Holy Spirit was poured out in Acts chapter 2. @MarcusTankard #PrayerSecrets
- 🐦 The Holy Spirit comes to our aid in prayer by alleviating one of the greatest weaknesses: ignorance. @MarcusTankard #Prayer Secrets
- 🐦 Speaking in tongue can unlock operations of the Spirit for our lives, families, churches and nations. @MarcusTankard #PrayerSecrets

6 ADVENTURES WITH THE HOLY SPIRIT

Ephesians 6:14-18
Stand therefore, having girded your waist with truth, having put on the breastplate of righteousness, and having shod your feet with the preparation of the gospel of peace; above all, taking the shield of faith with which you will be able to quench all the fiery darts of the wicked one. And take the helmet of salvation, and the sword of the Spirit, which is the word of God; praying always with all prayer and supplication in the Spirit, being watchful to this end with all perseverance and supplication for all the saints.

If you ever attended Sunday school as a child, I'm pretty sure that your teachers covered the armor of God. The church my family attended at the time had the children make costumes with the belt of truth, breastplate of righteousness, shoes of peace, the faith shield, the helmet of salvation and the sword of the Spirit (the word of God). We had fun as we left Sunday school with these costumes made out of cardboard taped all over our church outfits. I remember being convinced that with this armor I could beat up on the devil any day of the week.

But there's one thing that my Sunday school teachers didn't teach me about the armor of God. No one told me where or how to use the armor properly. The older I got, the more I learned how to read the scriptures in context for myself. If you delete verse 18 out of Ephesians 6, you remove the purpose of the armor of God from the chapter. If you don't know the purpose of the armor, then you will inevitably abuse it.

Paul makes it quite clear in verse 18 that the proper place for using the armor is prayer. He gives a very direct command to stand! In the previous verses he talks of how the days are evil and you'll have to make a persistent effort to stand and be strong in the Lord. If you don't stand then you run the risk of the devil taking advantage of you.

How do you stand? By properly placing the armor of God in your life. Arming yourself with the truths of the word like of who you are in Christ, knowing how to walk in the peace of God, and being strong in faith all work together to make you strong in spirit and strong in mind. But where are you standing? In prayer.

Praying Always

The believer is called to a life of prayer. There isn't a special calling to pray. All of us have been given the same access to the throne of God. Every believer has an audience with God to make their petitions, worship, and pray for other people. Not all believers utilize this privilege, therefore some people get more results in prayer than others. Prayer is like anything else in life; the more you do it, the better you become at it.

We aren't just called to pray, we are called to be in constant prayer. Paul says we are to pray always. That means that when you aren't talking to people, you should be talking to God. This is what I call *practicing the presence of God*. It's where you train your mind to bring your attention back to God so there is a consistent flow of fellowship.

In the Spirit

Paul says that we are to pray always "with all prayer and supplication in the Spirit." Many times when you see the phrase praying in the Spirit or praying in the Holy Ghost, it's talking about praying in other tongues. But that can't be what he's talking about here because we can't pray every prayer in tongues. You don't pray the prayer of faith in tongues. When you present your petition to God, you pray specific scriptures about a specific circumstance. You don't need the Holy Spirit to give you utterance for the prayer of faith. If you're going to cast your care on the Lord, you can't pray that in other tongues. Casting your cares on the Lord requires that you communicate the care to the Lord, not push the responsibility off on the Holy Spirit. Remember the Holy Spirit doesn't do the praying for you; he's there to help you pray.

In this instance, praying in the Spirit is more than just praying in tongues. Paul is not asking us to pray every prayer that we pray in other tongues. He's saying to pray every prayer *in the Spirit*.

Galatians 5:16
Walk in the Spirit, and you shall not fulfill the lust of the flesh.

Here's that phrase again in Paul's writings. He tells the Christians in Galatia to *walk in the Spirit*. Does that mean he was telling them to walk in tongues? Absolutely not. He's instructing them to conduct their way of life *in the Spirit*. In the Spirit is a place where you are more conscious of the Holy Spirit than you are of your external circumstances. When you walk in the Spirit, you're not walking according to your flesh, traditions of men, or the culture of the world. You disconnect from all of that and you hook up with God's will and His way of doing things. As the Holy Spirit distributes God's heart to yours, you walk out His desires. God's thoughts become your actions because the Holy Spirit is conveying His desires to you and you are responding with obedience.

What does that have to do with prayer? It has everything to do with prayer. Paul says to us, "Praying always with all types of prayer and supplication in the Spirit." In essence Paul is saying to us, "No matter how much you learn about prayer and no matter how much you have prayed, bring everything that you know and everything you've experienced in the Spirit. Let every prayer that you pray flow from the leadership of the Spirit. Settle it firmly in your heart that you will not follow your own agenda in prayer. Determine to find out what the Spirit wants to pray and pray that and only that."

Praying in the Spirit is more than praying in tongues. It's praying under the leadership of the Spirit. You don't even pray in tongues without the Holy Spirit leading and prompting you. The Holy Spirit didn't fill you so he could take a back seat to your prayer life. He wants to inspire utterance and direction in prayer.

Prayer Lists

This is why I don't generally pray with prayer lists. Some people can work with prayer lists. But I have never been able to use one effectively and I've tried it many times. I would make my list of requests and my short list of people who I wanted to pray for. Because people ask for prayer a lot, my list was quite long when I coupled their prayer requests with my own. Compiling a list was never the issue; sticking to the list was the problem. Sometimes I'd begin praying over the items on my prayer list only to find that the first few items got most of my attention. After the fifth or sixth thing on the list I was tired and I'd say, "Do it Lord and I'll say you did! Amen."

The other thing that commonly happened was I'd get distracted by a desire to pray a certain thing or pray for something completely different than what was on my list. It would seem like my desires would shift as a pray. I didn't realize at the time it was the Holy Spirit speaking to me through the desires of my heart to pray along a certain line. I would get sidetracked only to find that my little "rabbit trails" in prayer were occupying most of my prayer time.

My problem with prayer lists is that they don't always reflect the leading of the Spirit. Prayer lists tend to reflect what you deem necessary to pray about at the time. But your assessment of the problem isn't always accurate or God-inspired. Sometimes we must allow our minds to collapse into our spirit. What do I mean by that? I mean that we must allow our mind, will and emotions to detach themselves from our prayer time and allow our hearts to tune in to the Holy Spirit within us. Sometimes this requires prayer. Praise and worship is a good way to turn our focus inwardly. Our hearts tend to soften as we reflect on the goodness of the Lord and worship Him for all that He is to us. Another way to get your heart in tune with the Holy Spirit is to pray in tongues. Allow your spirit to be edified and launched into a new awareness of His presence. It's from this place of awareness that direction and utterance flow freely in prayer. All this takes place without the restrictions of a list.

Sometimes you'll find that the very thing you think needs the most prayer doesn't need a lot of attention at all. Maybe you need to confess the Word or just thank the Lord for working it out. Being in the Spirit when you pray helps to fix your perspective so you aren't praying about things you should be praising God for working out in advance.

It's not until we get in the Spirit that we can clearly see what the Spirit wants to pray about and how he wants to pray about it. My reasoning is that the Holy Spirit is aware of every one of my needs as well as the needs of others represented on any list I compile. He is not only aware of what is on my heart to pray about, he knows what prayer will bring the desired result. So if I come into prayer and submit my desire and prayer lists to him, he will inspire me to pray the perfect prayer for the situation.

Praying in the Spirit ensures that you are praying the will and way of God over the situation. It requires you to pray out as far as you can with what you know to be God's will. Take the scriptures that you have on the situation and pray them out to God declaring what you know to be true. Then begin to search your heart and pray as the Spirit leads you. This includes praying in tongues, but it most certainly is not limited to praying in tongues.

I'm not advocating that you don't pray with a list. If praying with a list works for you, do it. Just don't allow your list to keep you from watching for the leading of the Spirit in prayer. The Holy Spirit was put on the inside to be followed. He may inspire you to pray about something or someone that is seemingly completely disconnected from the problem at hand. There is more to getting your prayer answered than getting what you want. Trust that God knows what the effect of your obedience in prayer will do. If it's what the Spirit is calling for, it will definitely bring you into profit, progress and prosperity (1 Corinthians 12:7).

God's Mouthpiece

When you allow the Holy Spirit to pray through you, he can use your mouth to declare the will of God in the earth. God's word in your mouth is just as powerful as God's word in His mouth. Jesus instructed us to pray "thy kingdom come, thy will be done on earth as it is in heaven." Our job then is to allow the Holy Spirit to bring the will of God as decreed in heaven to our spirit so we can declare it to be done on the earth. As we declare the word of God, the same power that was released at creation is released over the situations we are praying about. The realm of the spirit responds to the word of the Lord because someone lifted up their voice in obedience to God and spoke what He has already said.

Watching and Praying

Ephesians 6:18
Praying always with all prayer and supplication in the Spirit, being watchful to this end with all perseverance and supplication for all saints.

How do we pray in the Spirit? How

do we disconnect ourselves from the problem and turn our eyes inward to see what the Spirit is saying about the problem? We find our answer in the same scripture. Paul says we are to pray all prayer in the Spirit while *being watchful*. Don't just be watchful; be watchful with all perseverance. That means to be aggressively militant in your watching.

Where are we supposed to watch? Your attention should be fixed on the Holy Spirit. And where does the Holy Spirit live? In you. The cues that he's going to send you are in your own heart where he lives. The Holy Spirit is not a ventriloquist. He's not going to throw His voice or His leading somewhere else. He's living in you so he's going to lead you from the inside. So watching in the Spirit is an internal dialogue that takes place between you and the Holy Spirit as you pray.

Habakkuk 2:1 AMP
I will stand at my guard post and station myself on the tower; And I will keep watch to see what He will say to me and what answer I will give [as His spokesman]…

This scripture paints a beautiful picture of what it means to pray in the Spirit, or pray being led by the Spirit. Habakkuk was distressed about the children of Israel. But rather than come into the presence of God and hurl accusations and complaints, he settled himself. He said, "Rather than spouting off at the mouth, I'm just going to stand here in the Spirit and watch to see what He will say in me. And then from that place, I will proceed to speak."

We can be so ready to pray, that we can find ourselves praying without the assistance of the Spirit. Never ever pray independent of the Holy Spirit. Remember, he's the one who makes all of this work. He knows the future better than you know the past, so he's a trustworthy guide in the arena of prayer.

Discipline yourself to expect the leading of the Spirit in prayer. The strength of prayer is measured by your ability to pray with the Spirit. A great way to remember how to be watchful in prayer is to review the instructions we give children when crossing the street. Once a child reaches the corner of a street, we instruct them to stop, look both ways and listen to see if they hear any vehicles approaching. If they don't see or hear anything coming, proceed to cross the street (unless there are signs or signals telling them to do otherwise).

We can take this approach in prayer. When you are praying, to make sure you're still connected to the move of the Spirit in you, stop, look on the inside and listen. Sometimes you may need to pray in tongues a little bit to bring your attention inward to see if the Holy Spirit has something to say. That's ok. Spend as much time as you need going back and forth praying in tongues and praying in English. This is called praying in the Spirit. The Holy Spirit was given to help you do this great work of God. Rely on His assistance and respond to His assistance. The strength of your prayers will be measured by your ability to recognize and respond to what the Spirit is leading you to do and say in prayer.

When you pray in the Spirit, you become more aware of His leading than would if you had of been praying in your flesh. What does it mean to pray in the flesh? It means to pray without the assistance of the Spirit. Some of us know the word of God very well. But that's not an excuse to pray without the assistance of the Spirit. You can know how to pray, but not know what to pray (Romans 8:26). This is why and uncompromising reliance on the Holy Spirit is not optional. It must become away of life and be ingrained in the culture of our praying.

Recognizing the Leading of the Spirit

Most people miss out on the leading of the Spirit in prayer because they don't recognize His manifestation. Whenever the Spirit of God manifests, it is an expression of His desire to help and assist us in whatever we are doing. So when the Holy Spirit begins so express himself in you as you pray, its only because he desires to help you pray more effectively. He is an expert in the protocol of heaven and the plan of God, so the help that he brings will always be needful.

John 16:15
All things that the Father has are mine. Therefore I said that He will take of mind and declare it to you.

John 16:15 AMP
Everything that the Father has is mine. That is what I mean when I said that he [the Spirit] will take the things that are mine and will reveal (declare, disclose, transmit) it to you…

In this scripture, Jesus conveys to us how the Spirit will lead us in prayer and every other area of our lives. If you can follow the Spirit in prayer, you can follow him anywhere. Remember, the Holy Spirit leads us from the inside out. And he does it by declaring, disclosing and transmitting revelation through our Spirit.

1 Corinthians 2:9-10
But as it is written: "Eye has not seen, nor ear heard, nor have entered into the heart of man the things which God has prepared for those who love him." But God has revealed them to us through His Spirit. For the Spirit searches all things, yes the deep things of God.

1 Corinthians 2:9-10 AMP
But just as it is written [in Scripture] "Things which the eye has not seen and the hear has not heard, and which have not entered the heart of man, all that God has prepared for those who love him [who hold Him in affectionate reverence, who obey him, and who gratefully recognize the benefits that he has bestowed]." For God has unveiled them and revealed them to us through the [Holy] Spirit; for the Spirit searches all

things [diligently], even [sounding and measuring] the [profound] depths of God [the divine counsels and things far beyond human understanding.

We should expect the Holy Spirit to declare things in our Spirit as we pray. Paul paints such a vivid picture of how the Holy Spirit conveys revelation to our Spirit. As you pray in tongues, the Holy Spirit diligently searches all things pertaining to the things you're praying about. Then he begins to give voice and expression to the divine counsel of God beyond what your mind can even begin to comprehend. He conveys this to your spirit in other tongues, spontaneous leadings or impressions to pray along certain lines, bringing scriptures to you to pray over a situation and a myriad of other ways.

Declaring

I remember when my dad was in need of another building for their church in Murfreesboro, TN. At that time, he was having two services in a small building and had considered starting a third service. He asked the prayer department to begin praying about another location. As we began to pray about the next step for our church, I found myself praying in tongues about the next property a lot. Even after our prayer group would meet, I'd find myself with a strong desire to pray about it later in the day. I remember praying in tongues about the church on my way to work one day, when I heard two words intermingled in my tongues: main street.

The Holy Spirit was giving me utterance to speak, and because I'd connected my lips to my spirit, I wasn't actively thinking about every syllable escaping my lips. I just hooked up lips to the flow of prayer coming through my spirit. As I did that, I noticed that there was a series of syllables that I kept repeating. It wasn't long that I noticed that I was kept repeating who words that sounded like *Main Street.* I wasn't thinking about Main Street at all. These words were coming out of my mouth without my permission or conscious effort. As far as I knew, I was just speaking in tongues as the Holy Spirit gave me utterance.

I responded to what was happening to me in prayer by saying, "Yes Lord I hear you. I lift up Main Street. Thank you Lord for Main Street." The more I prayed over those two words, the more they grew in my heart and the more urgency I felt to pray. This is where unskilled pray-ers can get in trouble. When you can sense the Holy Spirit leading you in prayer, it's easy to turn what the Holy Spirit is inspiring you to pray into a "prophecy" and say, "The Lord is saying…" Just because you are led to pray a certain direction doesn't mean God wants you to turn that prayer into a prophecy. We see and know in part. God is not telling you to prophesy to anybody; he's inspiring you to pray.

The temptation was to call my dad and have him look at all the properties on Main Street in Murfreesboro. But that's not what a skilled prayer does.

Don't turn a cue in prayer into a concrete direction. Be led by the Spirit, not a cue you've received in prayer (Romans 8:14). I resisted the temptation to call my dad and continued to pray. Before I reached my destination, I heard these words real strong in my spirit, "The church is on the main street." What was happening? The Holy Spirit was declaring something in my spirit for the purpose of me praying it out loud. Recognizing the leading of the Spirit, I declared this phrase out of my mouth over and over again until I sensed I was finished praying.

I don't recall praying that way about the church ever again. A few months later I moved to Tulsa, Oklahoma to attend Bible school. One day after classes I got a call from my dad saying they had bought an old Baptist church on one of the busiest streets in Murfreesboro. The church was located on one of the main streets that run all the way through the city.

My point in sharing this story is not to insinuate that God gave my dad the new building because of my praying. I'm sure the Holy Spirit had other people praying about the new church building. And I'm also sure that the Holy Spirit led them in many different ways in prayer. I am simply trying to give you an example of how the Holy Spirit will declare things to you in prayer when you allow him to take the lead.

Disclose

Other times the Holy Spirit will disclose things to your spirit. The only way I can describe this is if I compare it to a dark room. When you walk into a dark room, the details of the room (furniture, carpet, closets etc.) are hidden from your view. But when you turn on the light, everything that was hidden from your sight is now revealed. The flow of the Spirit in prayer can be like this.

For example, lets say you are praying for your marriage. It is God's design that if you want to be married that you have a healthy, vibrant, and exciting marriage. But maybe over the years your marriage has become lifeless. As you begin to pray about your marriage, you cast your care on God. Casting your care on God would include you detailing everything that is on your heart concerning your marriage. You would talk about your love for your spouse (past and present). Express to God exactly what kind of fulfillment (emotional, physical and spiritual) that you would like to experience from your marriage and why. Pray out the scriptures in the Word concerning marriage and the roles of each person.

After you have poured out your heart and prayed the promises of God over your marriage, now its time to pray in tongues about it. This is where a lot of people disconnect in prayer. We think because we've shared our heart with the Lord and prayed a few scriptures that we are finished praying. It's good to pour our heart out to God and pray the Word, but you should, never end a prayer without actively looking on the inside to see where or how the Holy Spirit will instruct you to pray.

One of the best ways that I've found to do this is by spending a few moments praying in tongues. Speaking in tongues will edify your spirit in such a way that it will awaken your spiritual senses. Paul said that God is ready to reveal what your eyes haven't seen, ears haven't heard and what your heart hasn't conceived yet. When you speak in tongues, you release your spirit to see, hear and understand things that your intellect cannot calculate and receive.

As you begin to pray in tongues, you are releasing the utterances as the Holy Spirit gives them. These utterances you received are sounds and syllables that actually escape your lips in an unknown tongue. The Holy Spirit is now actively engaged in your prayer right down to the enunciation of your words. The more you speak in tongues, the easier it is to connect your lips to your spirit and release yourself to speak without the permission of your mind. You will step into a greater flow and expression of the Spirit when you release your inhibitions to him in prayer.

Your mouth is speaking in tongues as your spirit is receiving utterance. But what are you doing with your mind? Obviously you are watching for utterance as it springs out of your spirit. However, it wouldn't be a bad thing to grab a scripture and meditate on that as you pray over your marriage. Ephesians 5:25 tells husbands to love their wives as Christ loved the church. You can work that scripture as you pray in tongues. It will help to keep your mind from wandering as your spirit is praying.

As you are praying about your marriage in other tongues, suddenly the eyes of your understanding are flooded with light and you are able to see things in your marriage from a different perspective. Remember when you walk into a dark room, the particulars of the room are hidden from your sight. But once you turn the light on, everything comes into view. That's one of the ways that the Holy Spirit will lead you in prayer.

In this instance, he opens your eyes to see what's really lacking in your marriage is an extended time of vacationing for you and your wife. God begins to reveal to you the need for fun, rest, and relaxation. With the responsibilities of a career and parenthood, you and your spouse have grown apart. A time of vacationing will provide you an opportunity to reconnect and refocus your life and marriage on God's plan.

Now is not the time to stop praying. You started praying about the marriage, and then God revealed to you what was needed. Don't leave prayer and try to create something based on a glimpse that God gave you. When you receive insight in prayer, lift it back up to the Lord in prayer. Begin to pray about what He told you. Something as simple as, "Lord I thank you for that. I can see that clearly now. I ask you now to forgive me for my negligence in that area. Show me how to make this shift.

Cause wisdom, innovation and witty ideas to spring up on the inside of me concerning the next series of steps in my marriage."

Then go back to praying in tongues. The Lord may speak to you further concerning strategic ways you implement some things into your marriage, and He may not. The important thing is that you don't leave the prayer time until the Holy Spirit is finishing leading and speaking.

Transmit

John 16:13 AMP
But when He, the Spirit of Truth (the Truth-giving Spirit) comes, He will guide you into all truth (the whole, full Truth). For He will not speak His own message [on His own authority]; but He will tell whatever He hears [from the Father; He will give the message that has been given to Him], and He will announce and declare to you the things that are to come [that will happen in the future]…

Jesus calls the Holy Spirit the Spirit of truth or the Truth-giving Spirit. What does that mean? That simply means that the Holy Spirit will give your spirit truth. In John 17:17 says that the word of God is truth. So the Holy Spirit will feed scriptures to your heart and assist you in prayer. In other words, Jesus detailed how the Holy Spirit would bring truth to our spirits. He said, "He (the Holy Spirit) [will] bring to your remembrance all things that I said to you." This means that the Holy Spirit will take the truth of God's word that you've read, heard and studied and will transmit it to your spirit when you need it – specifically in prayer.

I can remember praying and confessing the Word over my finances. At the time I was in need of wisdom and strategy for the next phase of my life financially. So I confessed the Word and began to pray in tongues. As I'm praying, I saw these words flash across my spirit: The Lord is my shepherd and I do not want for anything. I remember thinking to myself, "That's in the Bible somewhere." At that moment it dawned on me that the Holy Spirit was feeding my spirit more ammunition to use in prayer.

So I lifted up my voice and said, "Father I thank you that you are my shepherd and I do not want. I will not lack for wisdom, I will not lack for opportunity and I do not lack for money." I said that over and over again; each time I could sense the anointing to pray getting stronger and stronger. A pattern began as I prayed in tongues, the Holy Spirit would give me scriptures to pray, and then I'd pray the scriptures he was giving me in English.

Getting in the Flow of Answers

When you get in the flow of the Spirit, you are in the flow of the answers. The Holy Spirit will begin to flood your heart with utterance to pray.

All you have to do is respond to His promptings. When the believers were first filled with the Spirit in Acts 2:4, they began to speak in tongues, as the Spirit gave them utterance. In other words, they responded to the prompting of the Spirit. Adventures with the Holy Spirit begin are predicated on your ability to hear and respond.

The flow of the Spirit entails not only supernatural utterance, but also wisdom, direction and even revelation. When you step into His flow, your spirit is released to express the reality of its nature. You are not a natural being having a spiritual experience. You are a spiritual being having a natural experience. In other words, while your body will die and fade away into dust, your spirit will live forever. When you pray in the Spirit, you release your spirit to function without the inhibitions of your body. You can commune with God on a level that your is familiar with.

Prayer is Supernatural

Revelation 8:3-5
Then another angel, having a golden censer, came and stood at the altar. He was given much incense that he should offer it with the prayers of all the saints upon the golden altar which was before the throne. And the smoke of the incense, with the prayers of the saints, ascended before the God from the angel's hand. Then the angel took the censer, filled it with fire from the altar, and threw it to the earth. And there were noises, thunderings, lightenings, and an earthquake.

This scripture gives us a picture of what happens when we pray with the Spirit. Our prayers don't just release the supernatural, our prayer are supernatural. The very words that we speak out of our mouths are the building materials for miracles, signs, wonders and the operations of God. Notice here that the angel took the prayers of the saints and offered them before the Lord with the smoke of the incense. Then the angel took fire from the altar and the incense and cast them to the earth.

When we lift up ours Spirit led prayers to the Lord, they return to the earth bigger than they left. In this scripture the angel took those words and the fire of God and thrust them out to many fronts. And what were once seemingly mere words of prayer came back to the earth as noises, thunderings, lightenings, and earthquakes.

I saw the reality of this scripture manifest while I attended Rhema Bible Training Center in Broken Arrow, Oklahoma. During the summer I started a small prayer group in my apartment. It began as just a few of my friends gathering to pray out the plan for our lives and ministries. But it quickly grew until we had over thirty people meeting in my apartment.

We relocated to a warehouse owned by a Rhema graduate in the city. On this particular night we had over a hundred Rhema students there. We gathered to pray about the coming school year, but I also had it in my heart to pray for Rhema graduates all over the world. So as a general rule, I would lead the group in prayer (in English) and then we would all pray in other tongues and follow the Spirit wherever he wanted to lead.

As we were praying in tongues, the Spirit of God came on me in a very tangible way and I began to pray out these words, "Don't give up! You can't stop now! There are people praying for you. You cannot quit! Stay in the boat." After the prayer time I didn't think anything of it. I remember exhorting the group to watch to see if the Holy Spirit would inspire them to pray for the Rhema, students and graduates throughout the week and we closed the meeting.

The next week, we picked back up on that prayer assignment to pray for Rhema. After we'd finished praying I asked how many new people were there. And there were a lot of newcomers most of which were Rhema grads. So I gave them an opportunity to introduce themselves and tell us how they heard about the group. The only one that took the opportunity to speak was a stocky Caucasian man.

He said, "I'm a missionary to Australia. Last week was the toughest week I've had on the mission field yet. I'd run out of money and my church was in a mess. I pray a lot while I'm in the shower. Before I left for the States, I told the Lord I wasn't going to return to Australia. But he spoke up on the inside and said, 'don't give up! You can't stop now! There are people praying for you. You cannot quit! Stay in the boat.' Tonight I am really encouraged."

Needless to say there was jumping, shouting and dancing all over the room. It was such a great confirmation to us that we were flowing with the Spirit as we prayed. The seed of obedience that we sowed in Broken Arrow, Oklahoma manifested a harvest of encouragement for a discouraged missionary in Australia. Manifestations of the Spirit belong to the believer who will hear and respond to what He is calling for.

Phillip Halverson once said that when the Holy Spirit brings phrases or words to your spirit in prayer, it is very important you lift those words up to the Lord. For example, if the word *pilot* comes to your heart while you are praying in the Spirit, the moment that you release that word, power and anointing is potentially dispensed to whatever carries the name *pilot*. Everything from the Pilot pen, to a pilot for a television show can be influenced by the power of those words. There could be a family with the name Pilot as a last name. Never allow your ignorance to keep you from flowing with the Spirit. He knows how all these things connect.

Before I went to Rhema, I spent a lot of time praying in tongues to prepare myself for the school year. As I prayed in tongues, I noticed that there were names integrated in my tongues. Seemingly without my permission names like *Opie*, *Amanda* and *Weddle* were escaping my lips. I took note of that and wrote it down in my prayer journal.

Within the first week of classes starting, I met a girl named Amanda who introduced a guy named Robert whose nickname was Opie. Within days Robert and Amanda introduced me to another guy named Logan Weddle. These three people became my best friends during my time at Rhema. In fact Robert was my best man in my wedding.

In my book Praying Out the Plan, I talk a lot about these types of operations in prayer. You have to pray out the plan so you can walk it out. God doesn't tell you everything at once. But as He gives you a glimpse here and there, you'll begin to see patterns in your prayer times. It's not for you to put your own interpretation on the cues that you're receiving in prayer. God doesn't need your assumptions; He only needs your faith. Keep the switch of faith turned on by continuing to pray with the Holy Spirit.

I didn't go to Rhema looking for women named *Amanda*. I simply kept what I'd received before the Lord and in my prayer journal. When I finally did meet the people I'd been praying about, it served as a confirmation to me that I was following the Spirit in my prayers and that I was on the right track. When you're confident that you're hearing from God, it will inspire you to give your self more intentionally to the flow of the Spirit in prayer.

The Realms of the Spirit

The possibilities are endless when you are on an adventure with the Holy Spirit. Determine to be led by the Word and the Spirit. Don't try to re-create any of the testimonies in this book. I've shared these things with you to inspire your faith and show that there's more available to you than what you may have experienced thus far.

Renew your mind to the truths that have been shared in this chapter. They will enlarge you ability to receive from the Holy Spirit. Then as you are praying, be careful to not put your interpretation on what you receive from the Holy Spirit. These prayers are in the Spirit and so you will see their manifestation come by the Spirit, not your flesh.

Some people have endeavored to mimic other prayers that they deem to very spiritual and they have gotten off base in prayer. Someone else's experience is not your standard for prayer. Jesus is our standard for successful prayer. When we study the prayer life of Jesus, he was so skillful that he prayed about things that haven't even happened yet. We are still waiting on the manifestation of some of the things that he prayed. His prayer life was so powerful that the words that he spoke are still affecting His followers thousands of years after His death and resurrection. But Jesus was very clear that we are to live our lives based on the words that proceed out of the mouth of God.

If you want your prayer life to be on fire with operations of the Spirit, then you have to make sure that you are on fire with the Word of God. Jesus called the Holy Spirit the Spirit of truth. I like to say that the Holy Spirit will only land on the Word. What do I mean by that? It means that the Holy Spirit will only endorse prayers that are based on the Word. If your praying isn't based on the Word of God, then the Holy Spirit is not obligated to honor it with His presence or His help.

To keep this from happening, you should read the Word more than you pray. This will ensure that your praying is not going beyond the boundaries of the Word. NO matter how spectacular an experience in prayer is, if it doesn't agree with New Testament doctrine, then it's not okay. You can only flow with the Spirit to the extent that your mind is renewed with the Word. A renewed mind is a mind that agrees with God. When you and the Holy Spirit can agree on what God has said, then you can flow with what God has said and see His plan manifested in your life and in the lives of those you are praying for.

Stay Balanced

Balance is the key. I've seen so many prayer people get off base in this area. God will show them things in prayer and they move out to do things that God didn't author. God may show you things in prayer about people. But that's not for you to turn it into a conversation with someone else. If you do, God will stop talking to you.

I remember there was a particular minister that I had been praying for and one day the Lord spoke to me and said, "All of their children smoke marijuana." I was shocked when I heard it. "Why are you telling me this? Do you want me to talk to them?" I asked. He said, "Absolutely not. I'm telling you this so you can pray and so you won't allow emotion to overtake you when it becomes public."

If I had of took what I knew about those children and told their parents, I would have grieved the Spirit. God never told me to contact the parents or the children. He said, "Pray." If God says pray and I do something else, there's a word for that: sin. Sometimes good intentions are simply sin cloaked with concern. Revelation doesn't authorize a prophetic utterance. Wait on the Lord. If He needs you to say something, He will tell you the same way that He showed it to you. Otherwise, keep it before him in prayer. Don't be presumptuous.

We must handle these things delicately. There are things that God will move on you to pray about that could be potentially embarrassing if someone else found out about it. I think it's a wonderful thing that God can move on someone to pray for me about a weakness that I have without revealing my identity. If the individual follows the Spirit to pray, I will experience freedom. On the other hand, I need to exercise the same discretion when the Spirit of God moves on me to pray. Instead of asking questions and going on a fishing expedition, just pray and allow God to deal with the details. This is grace that covers sin while people are receiving the grace of God to come out of bondage.

Review Questions

1. Why were you given the armor of God?
2. What does it mean to pray in the Spirit?
3. List three ways the Holy Spirit leads us in prayer (Hint John 16:13)

Tweetable Moments

- When you get in the flow of the Spirit, you can get in the flow of the answers. @MarcusTankard #PrayerSecrets
- The strength of prayer is measured by your ability to follow the Spirit. @MarcusTankard #Prayer Secrets
- Most people miss out on the leading of the Spirit because they don't recognize His manifestation. @MarcusTankard #PrayerSecrets

7 CORPORATE PRAYER

2 Chronicles 7:14
If my people who are called by my name will humble themselves and pray and seek my face, and turn from their wicked ways, then I will hear from heaven, and will forgive their sin and heal their land. God calls His people over and over again into a place of prayer – not just individually, but collectively. The results of a collective supply of prayer are far reaching not only for the people offering the prayer, but the nations.

Many people are self-conscious when they pray alone, so it's easy for them to be people-conscious when they pray with others – specifically at a church meeting or prayer group. It's perfectly ok to be nervous about praying with other people. Some Christians feel the same way about attending church services or being a part of a small Bible study or discipleship group. All of these things require a certain level of vulnerability. But believe me when I say that the benefits of corporate prayer far outweigh the inhibitions we may have to pray with other people.

I sincerely believe that there is a special manifestation of God that we can enjoy and receive from when we assemble together with other believers. It is a manifestation that we don't receive on our own. This is why Hebrews 10:25 tells us to "forsake not the assembling of the ourselves together." God has something that He wants to do in our hearts when we come together. Our church gatherings provide an opportunity for Him to do just that.

For the most part I think we are accustomed to coming to church to receive something from God. But most of us don't come to church with "work" on our brain. We don't come with the intention of working with God or working for God. But this is exactly what He has on His mind. God wants us to work with Him in prayer so His plan can be manifested in our families, churches and nations.

A Praying Church

Luke 19:45-46
Then he (Jesus) went into the temple and began to drive out those who bought and sold in it, saying to them, "It is written, 'My house is a house of prayer,' but you have made it a 'den of thieves.'"

Jesus went to the temple and was appalled at the merchandising that was taking place in the name of God. I don't believe that the merchandise was a sin in and of it self. It's when the focus shifted from the primary purpose of the temple's existence that the problem came in. When we turn what God has deemed as a holy thing into a "cash cow" that we milk for everything that we can get, we grieve him. While God has designed ministry to bring increase and profit, He never designed it to be for one person's profit or personal gain. This is what angered Jesus: He found people utilizing the temple to promote selfish interests and filthy financial gain. The merchants resorted to wicked and ignoble means to obtain money by ignoring the vision God put in place for His house: prayer.

We miss the crux of this message when we focus on the outrage of Jesus versus what motivated His outrage. The words that He shared afterwards revealed God's plan for His house: prayer. Notice that Jesus didn't say, "My house is a house of power." He didn't say, "My house is a house of healing." He didn't even say, "My church is a house of worship." Yet we have all these things in our churches. And while I believe that all these things are necessary, they are all short circuited if prayer is not the pulse of the church.

It is in this phrase that we find the supreme purpose of the local church. He says, "My house is a house of prayer." The priority of our churches must be prayer. And not just prayer but answered prayer. We should have a reputation for getting answers to prayers and seeing the lives of people in our communities changed.

In order for God's house to be a house of prayer, there must be praying going on in His house. Jesus got angry because when He got to the temple, He should have found people praying. Instead of people praying, everyone was selling and buying things. Distractions killed the destiny of the temple. People weren't processing the plan of God in prayer; they were pushing their own agendas.

We've got to get angry like Jesus did. I'm not advocating that we storm the local church and start tearing up tables and kicking over pews. But we've got to get angry enough about the lack of results in prayer to actually do something about it. We must shift our priorities (and even church visions) to accommodate the words of Jesus: "My house is a house of prayer."

What is Corporate Prayer?

For the purpose of definition, corporate prayer is the expression of faith from a collective body of believers concerning a request. It is a collaboration of faith and spiritual supplies that equal power being made available to affect a change in the situation being prayed for. The Bible teaches that there is power in agreement.

Deuteronomy 32:30
How could one chase a thousand, and two put ten thousand to flight, unless their Rock had sold them, and the Lord had surrendered them…

Matthew 18:18-20
Assuredly, I say to you, whatever you bind on earth will be bound in heaven, and whatever you loose on earth will be loosed in heaven. Again I say to you that if two of you agree on earth concerning anything that they ask it will be done for them by My father in

heaven.

These scriptures convey that when we pool our faith together with other believers, there is a dynamic expression of power that goes into effect. A covalent bond is formed that is unstoppable. Regions can be shaken, families can be brought back together, and nations can shift by the words released from a group of believers who believe God.

Let's Pray Together

Jesus wants His church to come together and pray. I believe that united prayer is like music to the ears of God. So there is a call that's going out from heaven to the body of Christ. It's a call to assemble together and pray. I hear a lot of talk concerning the power that the early church experienced. The miracles, signs and wonders in the book of Acts were the norm for the early church. Many of us crave the power and presence that the early church had, but we must do what they did: pray.

Acts 4:23
And being let go, they went to their own companions and reported all that the chief priests and elders had said to them. So when they heard that, they raised their voice to God in one accord and said…

Peter and John were put in jail because the religious people of their day were not impressed with the miracles that were taking place in their ministry (to say the least). In fact, they were furious that the people were listening to Peter and John's messages. After being let go, they went to assemble with the other believers to not only report what had happened, but also to pray. This is one of the prayer meetings in the book of Acts that provides precedence for our present day prayer meetings in the local church.

Without playing semantics with words, lets examine what happened when they prayed. It says that they raised their *voice*. It doesn't say that they raised their *voices*. We should pay attention to that. Corporate prayer is not a bunch of people gathering in one room and praying at the same time. While people are praying, but its not corporate prayer as expressed in this scripture.

Corporate prayer implies that there is an assembling that has taken place. There is a difference between gathering and assembling. When we purchased nursery furniture for my son, most of the items came with an instruction manual that began with these words: Some Assembly Required. I couldn't gather all the parts and hope something comes out. If the furniture was going to resemble what was on the box and be useful to our nursery, I had to complete the instructions and assemble the furniture.

When you assemble a piece of furniture, every piece has a distinct place. Every part that comes in the box has a distinct function that only that part can fulfill. It's no different with corporate prayer. We can't just gather, pray and hope something clicks and we get manifestation. We must assemble. That includes everyone coming together to give a prayer supply concerning the same thing, at the same time and in order. When believers come together to pray this way, all of our voices come together as one voice to make one prayer to one God.

But we can't lift up one *voice* if we aren't in one accord. Focus is the key. When we come together to pray corporately, we can't have fifty different people praying about fifty different things at the same time. That's not once voice and that not praying with on accord.

When you build a fire, all the materials have to be in one place. As we assemble to prayer, all of us represent a unique prayer supply for the meeting. We must bring our entire supply (spirit, soul and body) into the service and submit it to the prayer focus for that time. We are not on one accord if we have assembled to pray for the nation, and I'm in the corner praying for my family. It doesn't mean that my family doesn't need prayer and that God doesn't love my family. But what it does mean is that we have assembled together to pray with one voice and with one accord. Too many prayer focuses in one meeting makes for too many voices. The power of corporate prayer is found in the *voice* that we make when we add our faith together.

The results to this time of prayer in Acts 4 were astounding. If you will read through the remainder of that chapter and the first half of chapter 5, you will see that God's poured His Spirit on the church again. They were able to speak with boldness, reverent fear fell on the entire church and miracles and healings earmarked that era. All because the people made corporate prayer a priority.

For the remainder of this chapter, lets examine some basic corporate prayer dynamics. I believe it is God's desire to draw us into a place of united prayer where we can bring heaven's supply through our churches and into every sphere of our societies (entertainment, politics, economies, etc.). As we cover these topics, allow them to sink down in your heart and paint a picture of what effective corporate prayer looks like.

Prayer Focus

If you come together to pray and you have nothing in particular to pray about, that's probably exactly what you're going to get: nothing in particular. There is nothing wrong with coming into a prayer group to just worship and wait before the Lord. But even out of that place of worship and waiting there is purpose. God is strengthening your inner man and satisfying you with His presence. So the time of prayer is never aimless. If you're coming to seek the Lord through a time of worship, that needs to be communicated. The problem comes in when there isn't a clear directive or purpose for the prayer time.

Proverbs 29:18 Amplified
Where there is no revelation, the people cast off restraint; but happy is he who keeps the law.

You've probably heard this scripture in reference to vision; whether its for your personal life, business or church. This can be applied to a prayer group. When people gather to pray but there are no clear directives or prayer points, there is nothing to restrain the group and maintain order. Order ensures that we are all moving in the same direction and pursuing the same result. Without order, any prayer request or inclination is free to be explored at the expense of legitimate needs that should be covered in prayer.

A prayer focus will ensure that you don't waste valuable corporate time praying about the personal needs of the people in the prayer group. There is nothing wrong with being a part of a prayer group with personal needs. The problem is when personal needs take up most of the prayer time at the expense of the prayer focus. The prayer group is not designed to minister to needs of the group members. From time to time, it may minister to group members. But ultimately, the goal of the prayer group is to bring a supply of faith and prayer to the prayer focus.

When you come to a prayer service, your goal should be to bring a prayer supply – not necessarily to receive prayer support. There are other avenues where you can receive that. Submit your prayer request to a group that accepts requests or that specializes in the area of your need. Maybe your church has a prayer group that focuses on finances. It would be perfectly in order to submit your request to the prayer leader and ask them to agree with you in prayer concerning your finances. (Be sure to give them scriptures that you are standing on before you ask them to agree with you in prayer). But to arrive at a prayer group whose focus is the presidential elections, for example, and expect them to derail their prayer focus to accommodate your need for prayer is out of order.

Let me be clear: having a need does not mean that you can't come to a prayer group. The point I'm trying to make is that the prayer group is not to be your personal prayer life. You have a responsibility to walk by faith and obtain personal victory for yourself. No one else can assume responsibility for victory in your life. You and only you must take it. The power of agreement in a prayer group will never alleviate your need to apply the principles of the Word for your own life. If you need help appropriating promises in the word of God, there are avenues to help you do so. But a prayer group is not designed to be that particular avenue.

If prayer groups don't possess a clear prayer focus, you will not know when you are getting results. We must become what I like to call "results-minded" as it refers to prayer. If we don't, we'll run the risk of doing a lot of spiritual things, but not getting concrete results in prayer. Remember, Jesus doesn't just want us to pray; he wants us to produce the fruit of answered prayer (John 15).

So if the prayer group is to pray for the pastor, then lets pray for the pastor. Let's not be found praying for neighbors, families and friends. It's not wrong to pray for these things, but we must cover first things first. The Holy Spirit will inspire prayer concerning the prayer focus that has been set for the prayer meetings. Should the opportunity be presented to pray for other things after the prayer group has covered the prayer focus, present your request and follow the prayer leader as the Spirit leads them. But remember: the prayer group is not to be your personal prayer life. So don't be upset when your personal prayer list is not a priority in a corporate prayer meeting.

Prayer Leaders

1 Corinthians 14:26
How is it then brethren? Whenever you come together, each of you has a psalm, has a teaching, has a revelation, and has an interpretation. Let all things be done for edification.

Effective corporate prayer has effective leadership. When we come together, everybody has a song, a revelation, a prayer directive, or a prophetic word. And this is a good thing! I believe that we should all come to the prayer meeting full of the Holy Spirit and the Word he's been teaching us throughout the week. But everybody can't give his or her latest revelation at every meeting. There must be someone in the group who can bring rhyme and reason to what the Spirit is saying and direct all the prayer supplies represented in the direction of the prayer focus that's been set in place. This is where the need for a prayer leader arises.

Without a leader in the prayer group, chaos is imminent. The leader ensures that we stay on task by keeping the prayer focus in mind. It is so important that the leader be someone who has developed their ability to follow the Holy Spirit because they are responsible for conveying Spirit-led directives for prayer to the rest of the group.

For example, the prayer focus for the particular group could be for the senior pastor of a local church. There are a lot of things that you could pray concerning a pastor. But a prayer leader will identify what the Spirit of God wants to pray about during that session and convey it to the rest of the group. Lets say, for instance, the Holy Spirit says, "Tonight, I want you to pray about the pastor's family." When this leading is expressed to the group, it's the group's responsibility to take up that directive and pray it out all the way until the end. What do I mean by *pray it out all the way to the end.* I mean that you draw utterance out of your spirit (in tongues and English) until the leader changes direction or the Holy Spirit stops leading.

It is so important how the leader

communicates the leading of the Spirit to the group. Without proper communication, the group members can't completely jump on board in faith to pray. Instructions for the prayer group should be clear and concise. The goal should be to communicate directives with speed, accuracy and clarity. Directives should never be given with a harsh tone. A leader should be firm, but the prayer group is not a dictatorship.

A short teaching on prayer is an opportunity to find the flow of the Spirit and pray what is on His heart. The best way that I've found to convey the leading of the Spirit for a prayer meeting is through Bible teaching and instruction. Prayer leaders should take fifteen to twenty minutes and share what they believe should be covered in prayer and how the group should pray about it. Faith comes by hearing the word, so scriptures should be paired with each point and directive so the group members can come to a place us faith and unity.

For example, if you were going to pray about the pastor's family, it would be perfectly ok to convey that to the group and then share some scriptures about family. If the Holy Spirit is leading you to pray in a particular direction, then there is a scripture that will help you pray. Scriptural precedence will enable the group to step into the flow of the Spirit by faith and maintain singleness of mind as you pray together.

A prayer leader should be of sound and disciplined mind. This individual should be well versed in the vision for the prayer group as it was communicated through the pastor or senior leader of the organization (unless of course they are the leader of that organization. I have led prayer groups for our ministry for years.) This is so important because the prayer leader is accountable to the senior leader for what was covered in prayer, how the group prayed for it, and the fruit that comes as a result of the praying.

We require that the prayer leaders in our church document what they prayed about, what scriptures they used in the prayer time, as well as the leading of the Spirit they had during the prayer times. These things are helpful to us as senior leadership because it ensures that the prayer group is staying on task. It is also exciting to be able to go back in our prayer logs and see the specifics the Holy Spirit was inspiring the groups to pray about after we see the manifestation.

Prayer leaders are also pivotal in keeping the prayer group etiquette in tact. This book is not about the prayer groups at our church, but I use our groups as an example because we are integrally involved in them. Our prayer groups have specific time constraints; most of them meet for one hour. We don't have a problem with them going over an hour, but if it is happening consistently, then we need to speak with the prayer leader and see why they aren't completing their prayer assignments in a timely manner. Prayer leaders diligently work to eliminate unnecessary conversations, presumptive chatter about the prayer assignment, excessive prayer requests that have nothing to do with the focus of the group and a host of other things.

Someone has to steward the flow of the Spirit in the prayer group. No one can control the Holy Spirit, but we can steward His flow. Being a good steward of his flow means that I take responsibility for its purity, so I don't allow a lot of ornamental praying and chatter to clutter the prayer time. If the prayer group is going to reach its highest potential, we have to be straight to the point and dismiss the prayer meeting.

Generally this means that the prayer leader will teach and update the group members for about twenty minutes. Then the group will worship or pray in tongues for a few moments. After everyone has got in the Spirit, we are ready to pray out God's plan for the prayer focus. Prayer will take place for the next thirty or forty minutes. After a brief review of what was received by the Spirit in prayer, the prayer leader will lead the group in thanksgiving and praise for what God did in the meeting and the group is dismissed. This is not a rule or "prayer group law." This is a basic outline for how prayer groups can keep their focus, and target their faith to reach their potential in their gatherings.

Any type of boundaries that are set by the pastor or the prayer leader are there to ensure that every group member experiences the flow the Spirit in prayer and joys of prayer. Where there is no vision for the prayer time, no one knows when the purpose of the group is fulfilled. Jesus wants your joy to be made full because of the fruit of answered prayer. When prayer leaders can guide their groups in the direction the Spirit is calling for, fruit will spring forth that inspire a greater commitment to a life of prayer – not just for the group, but for the individuals represented.

Keep Your Heart Right

Proverbs 4:23
Keep your heart with all diligence, for out of it spring the issues of life.

Many times when you see the word *heart* used in the Bible, it is referring to a combination of your spirit (the part that God lives in and leads you with) and your soul (mind, will, emotions, imaginations and intellect). God says to guard your heart because life flows from it. Jesus said that out of your belly would flow rivers of living water (John 7:37). You don't want to dam up the flow of the Spirit through you that was designed to be a blessing to nations of people.

One of the quickest ways to stop the flow of life in your prayer time is by harboring sin and iniquity in your heart. All sin is bad, but one of the more tolerable sins that you find among people of prayer is no walking in love. This can be for various reasons, but in most cases the reasoning behind offense in prayer groups is petty to say the least.

I knew a lady who left a prayer group because the prayer leader wouldn't allow her to share her latest revelation on tithing. The problem was that her revelation had nothing to do with the prayer focus. So to keep the group on task, the prayer leader didn't allow her to share her teaching on tithing. Remember, everybody who comes to the prayer group will have a song, a message, and/or a revelation. But the prayer group is not their platform to share that. If we are going to be effective in corporate prayer, we must stick to our prayer focus and not get distracted with doctrinal hobbies. Don't allow a petty offense like this one to keep you from being committed to a good prayer group.

Matthew 5:8
Blessed are the pure in heart, for they shall see God.

When you harbor unforgiveness in your heart, it will dull your senses to the anointing. Jesus made it quite clear that the pure in heart shall see God. We tend to interpret this scripture in light of seeing God in eternity. But I sincerely believe that our ability to maintain a pure heart is directly connected to seeing into the realm of the spirit clearly.

The only thing I can compare this to is music. As a pianist, I know the importance of playing music on a piano that's in tune. The worst thing that a budding musician can do is practice on a piano that is out of tune. Initially it may not cause a problem. But over a period of time, playing a piano that's out of tune will ruin your ear for tone, texture and pitch.

Sometimes when we have weak utterance in prayer, or can't seem to find a flow for the prayer meeting, it may be because some of the people present are allowing offense to govern their behavior. You were never instructed to be led by your feelings. God says be led by the Word and the Holy Spirit. Your physical and emotional senses will never give you permission to yield to God. If you're not yielding yourself to the Holy Spirit before you get to prayer, you don't magically learn to obey him perfectly just because you showed up to corporate prayer.

Your lifestyle has a direct affect on your ability to flow in a prayer group. Don't be the dead weight of the group. Handle your heart issues promptly by allowing the blood of Jesus Christ to cleanse every stain of sin – right down to the memory of wrong that was done to you.

Prayer leaders and groups have to be careful not to carry an attitude of elitism. When you are praying supernaturally, you will come into the knowledge of the news before it happens. Don't allow spiritual pride to set in. Never look your nose down at anyone because you perceive his or her prayer life isn't as exciting as yours. The truth is that we all have a lot of areas to grow in. So it pays to be humble as opposed to being a braggart.

Stay Hooked Up

There is an ebb and flow to corporate prayer. God didn't design prayer groups to be a place that we gather, pray as hard and fast as we can, poop out and then we go home. There may be times that we pray hard and fast, but that's not to be the standard for every prayer session. Our goal should be to identify what the flow of the Spirit is for that moment.

Sometimes I think we get sidetracked from the leading of the Spirit by trying to re-create experiences in prayer. The destination in prayer is the presence of God, but we may not take the same path every time. This week the prayer group may worship our way into the presence of God. The next week when we gather, we may pray in tongues until we all step over. Yet in another session we could confess the word until the power of God falls on us. And then there are times when we do nothing but wait silently before the Lord as His presence invades the atmosphere.

If you will follow the Holy Spirit, He will lead you into greater expressions of God's presence. But He can't do that if you are trying to re-create something that you previously experienced. Allow each prayer time to flow into its own uniqueness. When you follow the spirit, expect that. He is exceptionally good at the protocol of heaven.

Stay hooked up the entire prayer time. What do I mean by hooked up? I mean to be intentional about your thoughts. Pay attention to what the Spirit is doing in you and among you. I have seen too many people come into a prayer group, pray like a machine gun for twenty minutes and poop out. That's not how you do corporate prayer.

Develop the spiritual habit of watching in the Spirit. In a prayer group set your watch vertically and horizontally. Watching vertically means that you have your mind set to follow what the Spirit is saying to you (more accurately in you). There is an internal dialogue between you and the Holy Spirit where you have connected your mouth to your spirit. As the Holy Spirit voices utterances in (tongues and English), you release them without your mind inhibiting you. If you will fix your gaze on the move of the Spirit in you and through you, utterance will be a river that never runs dry. The Holy Spirit is the spirit of prayer and He will help you to pray as long as He has your attention.

To watch horizontally means two things: you watch the move of the Spirit through the leader and you watch how the group responds. Remember that this is corporate prayer. So you never pray independent of the other people in the group. It is never ok to disconnect from the group to pray about something else. Fight for your focus. Don't allow your mind to drift. Your prayer supply for the group requires your faith, prayer and attention. So don't get distracted with mental rabbit trails (i.e. problems on the job, family drama, or rumors you've heard).

As you pray with the group, you

should subconsciously submit what you are getting from the Holy Spirit to the prayer leader. Remember they are the one leading the group, not you. Your spirit may pick up on something as you all pray, but it may not be the direction that the leader wants to take the group. Don't be offended by that. What you say may be an assignment that you are to cover in your personal prayer time. Assignments like this are very important because they build you up and prepare you to travel further in corporate prayer.

Other times you have something from the Holy Spirit, and you don't realize that you have anything. A good prayer leader will draw that out of you. I remember praying with some people while attending Rhema Bible Training Center. We were praying about nations when the prayer leader looked at me and said, "Marcus you got it. Pray that out." I thought to myself, "Got what? What do I have?" She was drawing on a river of prayer in me that I wasn't conscious of.

She could tell I was very uncomfortable. So she coached me and said, "All you have to do is look on the inside. The Holy Spirit was placed in your heart to be followed. You can follow him." I thank God for good prayer leaders who know how to cultivate the gifts of the people in their groups. It encourages them to stay connected and grow in prayer. I did what she told me to do. Her reassuring words settled my fear (and embarrassment). Once I availed myself to what she discerned was in me, and looked on the inside, I saw that I did have something. There was an utterance in tongues in my heart just waiting on me to give voice to it.

As I began to speak and draw those words out of my spirit there was a rush of inspired utterance to pray in English. The more I prayed back and forth in English and tongues, a picture was being painted on my heart of a huge door. I turned to the prayer leader and said, "I see a door." "I see it too," she said. " Let's pray about it." So the group began to pray about a door. In the scriptures, doors can mean symbolic for many things (people, opportunity, a person's heart, for example).

As we prayed about the door, it was revealed to me that this was a door to China. We prayed about a door of utterance for China the rest of the prayer meeting. That moment relieved me of my inhibitions in prayer. It reminded me that I do know the Holy Spirit and I can follow him. But it took a prayer leader to draw that out of me and it took me staying connected to the group. When you allow your mind to wander, you miss out on promptings from the Spirit of God.

The key to staying connected to the group is always returning to your attention to your heart to see what the Spirit is saying. Return like the bird to the nest until the job is done. Don't allow your flesh to tell you when the prayer time is over. Stay connected by watching your heart and watching the prayer leader.

Don't be Too Chatty

When you pray in the Spirit, you pray being inspired by him. By definition, praying in the Spirit means to receive supernatural guidance from him in prayer. It is very exciting to experience the Holy Spirit convey the Father's heart to us as an authoritative voice, leading or unknown tongue. But you should be careful about putting your own interpretation on what He's saying to you.

Matthew 13:31,32
Another parable put forth to them, saying: "The Kingdom of heaven is like a mustard seed, which a man took and sowed in his field, which indeed is the least of all the seeds; but when it is grown it is greater than the herbs and becomes a tree, so that the birds of the air come and nest in its branches."

The crux of this parable is that the seed and the tree look amazingly different. Everything you receive from the Holy Spirit comes to you in seed form. Because the seed doesn't look like the tree it will eventually become, you should never make an opinion about the seed based on its current state. Seeds grow into big trees but not until someone plants them. How do you plant "seeds" in prayer? By praying!

When the Holy Spirit reveals something to you in prayer, sow it or give it back to him. Don't waste valuable time trying to analyze every little thing that you are led to pray about. Time spent discussing it, is time not spent sowing it. Once you sow it in the Spirit, it will grow and further revelation may come so you can pray it out further. But if further revelation doesn't come, don't try to fill in the blanks with assumptions. Simply write it down and trust God to manifest it as He sees fit. God doesn't always need your understanding as much as He needs your obedience.

Before I entered full time preaching ministry, I worked for a church in Oklahoma as a music minister. The pastor's wife was approached by one of the church members concerning something they had been praying. "The Lord told me you're going to have a baby!" The pastor's wife replied to her, "Thanks for praying for me, but I'm not pregnant and I don't have any plans to get pregnant." The next week, this church member approached her again with the same words, "The Lord told me you're going to have a baby." The pastor's wife was curious this time and said, "Why do you think I'm going to have a baby?" The person replied, "I've been praying for you and the Lord has had me praying for your baby. I've been praying out the word *mama* for the last few weeks. He even told me what you're going to name the baby: Courtney. You're going to name the baby Courtney."

This is where people who are given to prayer get it wrong. What this dear church member didn't know was that the pastor's maiden name was *Courtney*. So they probably were praying the mother of the pastor's wife. But speculation had this person draw up a narrative of the pastors having a baby.

Don't put your interpretation on the promptings you receive in prayer. Just leave it where you found it, in prayer. When God inspires you to pray along a certain line, it's not permission to turn it into a conversation. Sometimes prayer groups can get into error when they spend too much time trying to connect dots and break codes after prayer meetings. God's thoughts are higher than our thoughts and ways. Trust Him to manifest what He inspired you to pray without your mind understanding every detail of what you've prayed. Remember when you pray in the Spirit, your mind is unfruitful. That means that your mind will never be satisfied when you pray in the Spirit. These prayers originate from a place that your mind cannot find. So don't expect your mind to be satisfied. Instead, train your mind to not speculate and you'll keep the flow of the Spirit in your prayers clean.

Study More Than You Pray

The Word of God is the vocabulary of the Spirit. The Holy Spirit is the Spirit of truth. So the more familiar you are with truth, the more familiar you become with His voice. I cannot stress how important it is to stay in the Word of God. You must have a daily dose of the Word.

I have always loved to pray but I used to despise studying the Word. It seemed so boring to me. But the Lord changed my perspective on it when He compared it to fuel. I never complain about putting gas in my car. In fact, there's a gas station less than a mile from my house that I go to often. When I go to the gas station, I don't say things like, "I'm so bored with this gas. Every week it's the same thing." I don't require fascination with gas to fill my car up. In order for me to fulfill my duties as a family man and minister, I need fuel in my car. So I don't think twice about it.

We have to view reading the Word the same way. The Word of God is our "spirit fuel" for living. You don't get far in prayer or in your life without "spirit fuel." God said that "Man shall not live by bread alone, but by every word that proceeds out of the mouth of God." God's word nourishes and energizes your spirit so you can pray. Without it, your prayers lack the strength necessary to affect change.

Psalms 119:11
Your word I have hidden in my heart, that I might not sin against You.

God's Word provides an internal standard of living that governs our conduct. When we meditate on the Word, there is a stronghold of holiness and purity that is built in us that keep us on the straight and narrow path. This helps to safeguard us against hidden sin and iniquity.

Staying in the Word provides an

opportunity to expose every word and every thought to God. What's not needful can be disposed so it doesn't hinder the flow of your praying. When you are full of the Word, your prayers are quick and sharp. There is an edge that you have when you are full of the Word that someone who is just an occasional reader doesn't have. The reason for that is when you read the Word, you are communing with God. Prayer is you talking to God, but when you meditate on the Word, God is talking to you. Don't despise that communion because it will not just fuel your prayers – it will fuel every area of your life.

There are two subjects that I believe praying people should review regularly: who you are in Christ and the love walk. You can't pray effectively if you don't have a working knowledge of who you are in Christ. We must constantly be reminded of what God did for us when Jesus rose from the dead. The resurrection changed everything by paving the way into the presence of God for us all. I encourage believers to read what I call the General Electric Power Company (GEPC).

GEPC stands for Galatians, Ephesians, Philippians, and Colossians. These four books can be read individually within six minutes. I call them the power company because their focus is on the power of the resurrection in us, the lordship of Jesus Christ, righteousness, the authority of the church and many other truths that energize your praying. Take a colored pencil or pen, and underline every scripture that talks about who you are in Christ. Then confess those scriptures over yourself. Confessing the Word is another form of meditation. It takes the scriptures off the page and puts them into your heart.

You want your identity in Christ to be your default. When you pray, you will only go as far as your identity will allow you to go. You must believe that you've been made to pray. When you were born again, God didn't do a mediocre job. All things were made knew. God has made you able to see, hear and know in the Spirit. He has made you able to keep company with Him. Rely on the finished work of the cross in you and you'll see your inhibitions to pray melt away.

Stay Connected to the Local Church

One of the most important things I can stress to you as a praying individual is to stay connected to the local church. When you give yourself to prayer, your walk with God will take on an identity of its own. But that does not relinquish you of your responsibility to the local church. When Paul wrote letters to the churches in the New Testament, he spoke to individual people but he also spoke to the church collectively. While God doesn't just respond to the body of Christ as a mass ameba, there are still things that He has to say to local bodies of believers in a region.

Hebrews 10:24-26
Let us hold fast the confession of our hope without wavering, for He who promised is faith. And let us consider one another in order to stir up love and good works, not forsaking the assembling of ourselves together, as is the manner of some, but exhorting one another, and so much the more as you see the Day approaching

When you assemble with a local congregation, three things happen: you are strengthened in your faith, the God kind of love is stirred up and you are motivated to do wise decisions. Faith is your grip on God and it is strengthened when you are in an atmosphere where people believe the same thing that you do and are striving to know God and His Word. You should strive to be intricately connected to a church that strengthens your faith through biblical teaching and a clean flow of the gifts of the Spirit. The Word and the Spirit promote spiritual growth in the local church. Without it, you run the risk of walking in deception and not knowing it.

Ephesians 4:11-15
And he himself gave some to be apostles, some prophets, some evangelists, and some pastors and teachers, for the equipping of the saints for the work of ministry, for the edifying of the body of Christ, till we all come to the unity of the faith and of the knowledge f the Son of God, to a perfect man, to the measure o the stature of the fullness of Christ; that we should no longer be children tossed to and fro and carried about with every wind of doctrine, by the trickery of men, in the cunning craftiness of deceitful plotting, but speaking the truth in love, may grow up in all things into Him who is the head – Christ.

Jesus placed ministries in the body of Christ to help us to mature to a place of discernment. These ministers find their expression primarily in the local church. You cannot afford to disconnect from the church because there is a lush supply of spiritual food there for you. Without the maturity these ministries provide, you will fall prey to wicked and designing people with ungodly agendas.

One of the first ways that you can know that you are getting off course is that you start to separate yourself from the church. It may not be an abrupt separation. Generally is starts with comparisons. You begin to believe that you have access to spiritual things that others don't. This way of thinking tends to come out of an offense with the prayer group or a leader at the church who doesn't give heed to a revelation that you have. So rather than take correction, you internalize it as rejection and choose to believe that they are wrong and you're right.

You can't function properly separated from the local church any more than my hand can function properly separated from my body. The hand needs the body and the body needs the hand. Isolation is never the answer because it robs you of the supply you so desperately need. That supply in the local church is designed to furnish every area of your life. Value that supply enough to not allow deception to separate you from it.

When you are in church, there is doctrine that will keep you balanced in prayer. It's so easy to get off course in prayer. But the Word of God through your pastor and guest ministers in your church will keep you on the straight and narrow. The anointing teaches (1 John 2:20; 27)! The anointing in you teaches, but then the anointing on the minister teaches (Ephesians 4:11-15)! If you'll respond to both, you will have a proper checks and balance system for your prayer life

Review Questions

1. Why should believers assemble together?
2. What is corporate prayer?
3. Why is it important to stay connected to the local church

Tweetable Moments

- 🐦 Jesus was angry because when He got to the temple, He should have found people praying. @MarcusTankard #PrayerSecrets
- 🐦 Effective corporate prayer must have good leadership. @MarcusTankard #Prayer Secrets
- 🐦 We can't control the Holy Spirit, but we can be good stewards of His flow. @MarcusTankard #PrayerSecrets
- 🐦 When God inspires you to pray along a certain line, you don't have permission to turn it into a conversation. @MarcusTankard #PrayerSecrets

8 PASTORS, PRAYERS AND REGIONS

A substantial amount of a church's prayer life should be for the pastor and the region where the church is planted. Prayer is something that Paul asked for numerous times throughout his letters and it was undoubtedly because of the blessing that answered prayer brought to his ministry. Prayer initiates a chain of events that can lead to an invasion of the power of God in a region. In this lesson, lets examine the connection between prayer, the pastor and regions.

The Supernatural Gift of the Pastor

Ephesians 4:8-16 NKJV
When ascended on high, He led captivity captive, And gave gifts to men. (Now this, He ascended what does it mean but that He also first descended into the lower parts of the earth? He who descended is also the One who ascended far above all the heavens, that He might fill all things.) And He Himself gave some to be apostles, some prophets, some evangelists, and some pastors and teachers, for the equipping of the saints for the work of ministry, for the edifying of the body of Christ, till we all come to the unity of the faith and of the knowledge of the Son of God, to a perfect man, to the measure of the stature of the fullness of Christ; that we should no longer be children, tossed to and fro and carried about with every wind of doctrine, by the trickery of men, in the cunning craftiness of deceitful plotting, but, speaking the truth in love, may grow up in all things into Him who is the head Christ from whom the whole body, joined and knit together by what every joint supplies, according to the effective working by which every part does its share, causes growth of the body for the edifying of itself in love.

In Ephesians chapter four, Paul outlines what we call the five - ministry gifts of Jesus Christ. These are the ministries that Jesus placed in His church when He ascended into heaven. Jesus designed the ministry gifts to function as the present day expression of His ministry to the body of Christ. Pay very close attention to the wording: the present day expression of His ministry *to the body of Christ*. The five-fold ministry is not the present day ministry of Jesus. It's the expression of the present day ministry of Jesus to His body. There is a huge difference.

The body of Christ collectively is the present day ministry of Jesus in the earth. The global church was given the great commission to preach the gospel, heal the sick, cast out devils and make disciples. Everyone is called to preach the gospel in the entire world. But while the ministry gifts share in this commission, their ministry takes on a different nature based on Ephesians four. Paul says that one of the main functions of five-fold ministry is to equip believers for the work of the ministry. Therefore it is the job of the five-fold ministry to equip and impart to believers so they can reach their full potential in the ministry God has called them to in the great commission.

Paul listed five types of ministries in Ephesians 4:1 – apostle, prophet, evangelist, pastor and teacher. Each one of these gifts convey a ministry of Jesus Christ to his body and thus have an ingredient of the ministry of Jesus. The word pastor and shepherd are used interchangeable in the old and new testaments. So the pastor's ministry is an expression of the shepherd's ministry of Jesus Christ.

Feeding, Leading, Seeding

The pastor's ministry is one of feeding, leading and seeding. In the local church, that pastor delivers a well balanced meal of the Word into the hearts of the people who attend. Peter instructed believers to desire the sincere milk of the Word (1 Peter 2:2). When you crave the Word of God through the pastor, it cultivates a receptive heart to receive what is being taught. As you receive the Word of God, it is able to go into your heart and change the way you think, speak and act. The word of God is powerful and sharper than any sword (Hebrews 4:12), so it can uproot wrong thinking, deceptions, destructive patterns of behavior and a host of other things that may be inhibiting your progress in the plan of God. This is why the preaching and teaching ministry of the pastor is of utmost importance.

Psalms 23 paints a beautiful picture of the ministry of a shepherd. The psalmist paints the picture of God as a shepherd and the believer as a sheep. But seeing that Jesus is the chief shepherd and the pastor is the *under shepherd* we wouldn't do any harm by looking at the relationships between a pastor and his members.

Psalms 23
The Lord is my shepherd; I shall not want. He makes me to down in green pastures; He leads me beside the still water. He restores my soul; He leads me in the paths of righteousness for His name sake. Yea, though I walk through the valley of the shadow of death, I will fear no evil; for You are with me; Your rod and Your staff, they comfort me. You prepare a table before me in the presence of my enemies; You anoint my head with oil; my cup runs over. Surely goodness and mercy shall follow me all the days of my life; and I will dwell in the house of the Lord forever.

For the sake of this lesson, I want to focus on the leadership aspect of the shepherd in this scripture. The shepherd leads the flock. It's not enough for a minister to teach and preach the Word every week if the members of the church aren't being led into constructive spiritual progress in their personal lives. You can preach and teach the Word without leading the people. Leading requires that a pastor not just preach. If the ministry of a pastor consists of teaching, then that ministry is no different than the ministry of the teacher. While teachers are important to the body of Christ, the teaching ministry cannot replace the ministry of the pastor.

It is a shepherd's anointing that leads you from one place in life to another. A pastor's anointing won't just teach you how to get out of debt; it will lead you into financial overflow. The pastor's anointing can lead you into green pastures where there are opportunities, innovative ideas and witty inventions. Under the influence of the anointing in the local church, you can come into a greater revelation of your call as well as the supernatural relationships designed to propel forward.

As the shepherd feeds you the Word and leads you into places of increase, they also sow a vision for the world into your heart. It was never the design of God for the local church to be merely focused on itself. In fact, He told the disciples to lift up their eyes and give their attention to the harvest (John 4:35). It takes discipline to not allow yourself to get comfortable with church, and keep your heart set on reaching the lost. God loves the world; He's not merely tolerant of the world. He is so madly in love with the world that He gave His only son to die for their sin (John 3:16).

The pastor is anointed to sow a heart for the world into members of their church. In doing so, the believer can find their place in the harvest. As the pastor leads the flock towards the harvest, the entire region that the church is planted in can be influenced by the love of God and the gospel. This is how God has designed the local church to transform their communities. As the pastor downloads God's heart for their region, they convey this vision to flock through inspired preaching and teaching. As the Word of God is preached, the power of God flows and people's lives are changed.

Prayer Unlocks Heaven

We have studied the dynamics of how prayer works, but I cannot stress how important it is to be conscious that prayer is supernatural. The whole spirit realm moves by words. In fact, the universe that we enjoy today was put together by words. So when you yield to the Spirit to pray God's plan, those words are containers of the life and nature of God. Jesus said in John 6:63, "My words are spirit and they are life." His words don't lose power when you speak them. When you add your faith God's Word, anything is possible. The same power that's released when God speaks is the same power that is released when you speak His Word in faith.

God's Word contains God's power. His words are an expression of His power. So as we pray, we need to be conscious of the fact that we are moving power. With every word that is escaping our lips, we are affecting change in the realm of the spirit that will ultimately bring change in the natural realm. It is easier to add faith to our prayers when we are cognizant of what is going on as we are praying.

Acts 10:1-6
There was a certain man in Caesarea called Cornelius, a centurion of what was called the Italian Regiment, a devout man and one who feared God with all his household, who gave alms generously, and prayed to God always. About the ninth hour of the day he saw clearly in a vision an angel of God coming in and saying to him, "Cornelius!" And when he observed him, he was afraid, and said, "What is it lord?" So he said to him, "Your prayers and your alms have come up for a memorial before God. Now send men to Joppa, and send for Simon whose surname is Peter. He is lodging in with Simon, a tanner, whose house is by the sea. He will tell you what you must do.

Notice that Cornelius was a praying man. He had developed a lifestyle of praying and giving that so touched the heart of God, the angel said, "Your prayers and your alms have come up for a memorial before God." Simply put God was impressed with his praying and giving. The expressions of faith so moved God that it opened the realm of the Spirit to him to bring answers for his life. Up until that time, Cornelius had not heard the gospel. He didn't have the answer for salvation. But because of his faithfulness in prayer, those words so moved the heart of God that He provided a divinely granted appearance that revealed the first step to hearing the gospel message.

Prayer will unlock revelation for the next season of your life and church. But it takes people being committed to pray it out. What do I mean by pray it out? I mean to pray out the plan and purpose of God. When you do that, your words activate people, events, and strategies to be revealed and set in motion on your behalf. God will even begin to talk to other people who don't know you. He will begin to motivate them to bless and help you. This is exactly what happened to Cornelius. As the angel was speaking to him in a vision, God was providing a divinely granted appearance to a minister in another city concerning Cornelius and his family.

Acts 10:7-16
And when the angel who spoke to him (Cornelius) had departed, Cornelius called two of his household servants and a devout soldier from among those who waited on him continually. So when he had explained all these things to them, he sent them to Joppa. The next day, as they went on their journey and drew near the city, Peter went up on the housetop to pray, about the sixth hour. Then he became very hungry and wanted to eat; but while they made ready, he fell into a trance and saw heaven open and an

object like a great sheet bound at the four corners, descending to him and let down to the earth. In it were all kinds of four-footed animals of the earth, wild beasts, creeping things, and birds of the air. And a voice came to him, "Rise, Peter; kill and eat." But Peter said, "Not so, Lord! For I have never eaten anything common or unclean." And a voice spoke to him a second time, "What God has cleansed you must not call common."

Peter was one of the pioneers of the early church. When Jesus told the disciples to go into the entire world, he really meant it. But for the most part, the apostles had spent the bulk of their time preaching in the Jewish world. When Jesus came to die for our sins, he died for the sins of the entire world – every man, every woman, every boy and every girl. There was no discrimination in the blood of Jesus towards the human race. He died once, for all. As a Jew, Peter and the other disciples struggled to digest the global philosophy of the gospel and the love of God. This would ordinarily be a problem for someone like Cornelius because he was not a Jew. He was what was considered a Gentile: one who had no relationship or covenant with God.

The distinguishing mark about Cornelius was his faith. He prayed and gave alms willingly and consistently. And it was his faith-filled prayers that got the attention of God – much like the Syrophoenician woman got the attention of Jesus in Matthew 15:27. His faith filled words opened the spirit realm and unlocked a strategy to hear the gospel. But it also set things in motion for the man who would bring the message, Peter. This faith-filled prayer was so powerful that it unlocked a powerful revelation of God that challenged the ministry of Peter. In the vision, Peter sees an array of what Jewish believers considered to be unclean. The voice of the Lord thunders, "Rise Peter; kill and eat." Peter's response is typical of Jewish believers at that time, "Not so, Lord...I have never eaten anything common or unclean." The Lord spoke to him a second time and said, "What God has cleansed you must not call common" At the time Peter thought God was talking about food. But the reality is that God was talking about people. This story paints a beautiful picture of what happens when believers pray.

Acts 10:19-34
Now While Peter wondered within himself what this vision which he had meant, behold, the men who had been sent from Cornelius had made inquiry for Simon's house, and stood before the gate. And they called and asked whether Simon whose surname was Peter, was lodging there. While Peter thought about the vision, the Spirit said to him, "Behold, three men are seeking you. Arise therefore, go down and go with them, doubting nothing; for I have sent them. Then Peter went down to the men who had been sent to him from Cornelius, and said, "Yes, I am he whom you seek. For what reason have you

come?" And they said, "Cornelius, the centurion, a just man, one who fears God and has a good reputation among all the nation of the Jews, was divinely instructed by a holy angel to summon you to his house, and to hear words from you." Then he invited them in and lodged them. On the next day Peter went away with them, and some brethren from Joppa accompanied him.

And the following day they entered Caesarea. Now Cornelius was waiting for them, and had called together his relatives and close friends. As Peter was coming in, Cornelius met him and fell down at his feet and worshipped him. But Peter lifted him up, saying, "Stand up; I myself am also a man." And as he talked with him, he went in and found many who had come together. Then he said to them, "you know how unlawful it is for a Jewish man to keep company with or go to one of another nation. But God has shown me that I should not call any man common or unclean. Therefore I came without objection as soon as I was sent for. I ask, then, for what reason have you sent for me?" So Cornelius said, "Four days ago I was fasting until this hour; and at the ninth hour I prayed in my house and behold, a man stood before me in bright clothing and said, 'Cornelius, your prayer has been heard, and your alms are remembered in the sight of God. Send therefore to Joppa and call Simon here, whose surname is Peter. He is lodging in the house of Simon, a tanner, by the sea. When he comes, he will speak to you.' So I sent to you immediately, and you have done well to come. Now therefore, we are all present before God, to hear all the things commanded you by God." Then Peter opened his mouth and said: "In truth I perceive that God shows no partiality…

In obedience to the Spirit of God, Peter went with the men that Cornelius sent and when he arrived in Caesarea, God revealed to him the interpretation of the vision. This is so amazing because prayer sparked this chain of events. Cornelius was a praying man and his prayers opened heaven to him and to Peter. In Cornelius's vision, God revealed to him a strategy to hear a message that would change his life and the life of his family forever. I have heard many testimonies where people had dreams or visions where they were instructed to go to a certain church or a certain gospel crusade. When you do the research, you'll find that there was a series of prayers offered that set all that in motion.

The prayers of Cornelius didn't just unlock revelation for him - it also affected the preacher. This is what I want to focus on for the rest of this lesson. Because Cornelius was faithful to pray, Peter received a revelation that not only unlocked the next phase of his ministry it also brought the gospel to another region. As we pray faith filled prayers for our pastors, they will receive time sensitive intelligence from heaven that will open doors into nations, people groups and territories that were once closed. God opened a whole new sphere of ministry for Peter and then gave him utterance to speak a message that was custom made for the hearers.

The prayers that Cornelius prayed created a door of opportunity for Peter to preach to a completely different demographic. If God was calling your pastor to reach into a whole new demographic that the churches in your city had not influenced, would you be able to pick up on that in the Spirit and pray it all the way through into manifestation? Or are you content with just coming to church and doing business as usual? Would the Father's desire to reach the unchurched in your city pick up on the radar of your heart?

If so, then you are in a position to partner with God to pray out His plan for the expansion of your church. God will move on you to pray the vision of your church. Then as a result of your praying, heaven will open over your pastor and they will begin to see and know things supernaturally by the Spirit. They may not be able to explain everything that they are seeing or sensing in his spirit. But if you continue to pray, God will not only bring them into full disclosure of where the ministry is going, will also fill their mouth with a word that is custom for that demographic. Look at what happens as Peter begins to preach.

While Peter was still speaking these words, the Holy Spirit fell upon all those who heard the word. And those of the circumcision who believed were astonished, as many as came with Peter, because the gift of the Holy Spirit had been poured out on all the Gentiles also. For they heard them speak with tongues and magnify God. Acts 10:44-46

These people experienced an invasion of God's presence that would set precedence for Spirit-filled ministry. When Peter began to speak, there was such powerful utterance from the Spirit of God that no one needed to lay hands on these people to receive the baptism of the Spirit. Just hearing the Word of God opened their hearts so wide, that they received as Peter was preaching. These are the manifestations of the Spirit that I'm hungry for. I'm looking for the day when everyone in the service is healed before I can pray for the sick. I'm looking for the day when sinners flood the altars before we can give an appeal for salvation because the power and presence of God draws them to their knees.

This type of power is only witnessed when prayer is at the center of the church. God desires to do miraculous things in our midst. But prayer should be the fuel that makes our churches function properly – not programs and gimmicks. I'm all for a good project that's going to help minister to the needs of the people in the community. But projects and programs quickly become gimmicks and church growth schemes when they don't flow from a place of prayer and intercession for our pastors, churches and cities. God has given us an answer for our communities and its found in prayer.

Spiritual Warfare

I have heard a lot of discussion and teaching on the subject of spiritual warfare as it refers to praying for regions. But scripturally, I don't see the precedence for some of the spiritual practices that I've witnessed. If we are going to stay biblically balanced, we cannot afford to get carried away on doctrinal hobbies and tangents. When you compare scripture with scriptures, you can create boundaries that guard you from deception.

Rather than launch an attack on false doctrines, I have endeavored to just stick with the truth of God's Word and let the results outrun the excess, extremes and error in the church. As a Bible teacher, I know that giving clear direction as opposed to a harsh rebuke can cure most of the problems that we find in our churches. While rebuke will bring correction, it doesn't equip with the necessary tools to move forward in the right direction and safeguard believers from further deception. It is with this paradigm that I want to briefly discuss spiritual warfare.

The presence of the demonic over a region, people group or nation is not a new strategy. The devil has been exerting his influence strategically over territories for centuries. Evil spirits like to remain in certain locations in order to develop a stronghold that will keep the flow of the Word and the Spirit from reaching the people. We can see this in the ministry of Jesus in Mark 5.

Mark 5:9-13
Then He (Jesus) asked him, "What *is* your name?" And he answered him, saying, "My name is Legion; for we are many." Also he begged him earnestly that He would not send them out of the country. Now a large herd of swine was feeding there near the mountains. So all the demons begged Him, saying, "Send us to the swine, that we may enter them." And at once Jesus gave them permission. Then the unclean spirits went out and entered the swine (there were about two thousand); and the herd ran violently down the steep place into the sea, and drowned in the sea.

The spirits that were in this man had specifically asked Jesus not to make them leave the region. Why? It was because they had developed a stronghold in the city that up until Jesus showed up had been impenetrable. There's a lot to be learned from this passage. Demons like to hang out in certain parts of the world. They will seek out weak-minded people who will yield to them.

When some people think demonic activity, scenes from horror movies come to mind. The strategy of the enemy is simpler than that. Demon spirits will inspire wrong thinking in the minds of unbelievers and believers whose minds are not renewed with the Word of God. Paul ran into this with the churches in Corinth.

1 Corinthians 5:1-2
It is actually reported that there is sexual

immorality among you, and such sexual immorality as is not even named among the Gentiles – that a man has his father's wife! And you are puffed up, and have not rather mourned, that he who has done this deed might be taken away from among you.

History tells us that Corinth was culturally sexually immoral – much like what we see today in many cities. One of the territorial spirits at work in Corinth also influenced the thinking of the believers in the churches. The influence was apparently substantial because Paul addressed the immorality explicitly in his letter to the church. This clearly shows the effect of demonic stronghold over a city or nation.

This is why Paul exhorted the believers in Rome to not conform to the world's thinking and to allow themselves to be transformed by the Word of God (Romans 12:2). The prince and the power of the air dictates the affairs of the world (Ephesians 2:2), so we can't allow ourselves to be sedated by constant influx of imaging from our culture. We have to submit those things to God by allowing His Word to change our thinking. If left unchallenged, these people will find themselves opposing the move of God in a region.

2 Corinthians 10:4-5
For though we walk in the flesh, we do not war according to the flesh. For the weapons of our warfare are not carnal but mighty in God for pulling down strongholds, casting down arguments and every high thing that exalts itself against the knowledge of God, bringing every thought into captivity to the obedience of Christ.

In this scripture Paul outlines how the enemy works in the thinking of weak-minded people. It all begins with a thought. The devil will introduce a thought to you that is absolutely contrary to the Word of God and the will of God for your church and region. It could be over something as simple as a direction the ministry is taking.

Maybe the pastor has a vision to feed the hungry or build a youth center for underprivileged children. The enemy will find people who have a disagreeable personality - the people who are difficult to get along with for any number of reasons. He will use people who have been offended by the pastor's messages in the past. Or He could use someone who just isn't familiar with how church works to reach the lost in practical, innovative ways.

When people don't lend their minds to the will of God, it opens the door for the enemy to come in and fill their minds with all sorts of deceptive thinking. What begins as a thought quickly evolves into an imagination. Your imagination is the visual expression of your thoughts on the canvas of your mind. It's your imagination that takes a thought from your head and deposits it into your heart.

Once the enemy has introduced the thought and your imagination takes hold of it, it produces something called a stronghold. A stronghold is designed to oppose something; therefore a demonic stronghold opposes the Word of God. When we allow a way of thinking that is contrary to the word of God to dominate us and our communities, we effectively partner with the devil to build a stronghold that keeps the gospel from reaching the lost.

Paul says, "The weapons of our warfare are not carnal, but mighty in God for pulling down strongholds." You don't see Paul trying to fight the culture. The culture is not the root of the problem. Remember our fight is not with the flesh, it's in the spirit (Ephesians 6:12). The fight that we have to fight is a spiritual fight with spiritual weapons. The weapons that we've been given are the Word of God and the move of the Spirit.

When we can bring an undiluted flow of the Word and the Spirit into a region, it will outrun what the devil is trying to do in our communities and dismantle the strongholds of the enemy. This is why the enemy fights churches that preach the gospel and flow with the Holy Spirit: these churches are providing an answer for their communities.

The highest route to take in spiritual warfare over a region is to pray that God would send laborers with utterance and demonstrations of the Holy Spirit. This is how Jesus changes regions and it is the pattern that we see in the book of Acts. Bold utterance and demonstrations of the Spirit brought unparalleled revival in to cities like Samaria, Antioch, Ephesus and many others. But it was because the early church prayed and then saw the gospel preached and demonstrated with power.

1 Corinthians 2:4-5 NKJV
And my speech and my preaching were not with persuasive words of human wisdom, but in demonstration of the Spirit and of power, that your faith should not be in the wisdom of men but in the power of God.

1 Corinthians 2:4-5 AMP
And my language and my message were not set forth in persuasive (enticing and plausible) words of wisdom, but they were in demonstration of the {Holy} Spirit and power [a proof by the Spirit and power of God, operating on me and stirring in the minds of my hearers the most holy emotions and thus persuading them], so that your faith might not rest in the wisdom of men {human philosophy), but in the power of God.

Paul's ministry philosophy was the supernatural. He was not content with teaching the rhetoric of the day surrounding "the issues." He came preaching a message that was laced with the power of God. His preaching would spring from a place that the carnal mind wouldn't find. The sermon was an outward expression of an inward demonstration.

Paul would avail himself to the moving of the Spirit in his heart. As he did this, words would spring up in his heart and escape his lips that would bypass the intellect of the hearer. Enticing words and philosophies will satisfy the intellect, but they will never answer the hunger pangs of a man's spirit. So the words that Paul preached would outrun the arguments in the minds of the hearer and go straight to their spirits. Hebrews 4:12 declares that the word of God is alive, so these words entered the spirits of men with an assignment. The assignment was to stir up their most holy emotions.

What are most holy emotions? We know that we can have unholy emotions. You experience an unholy emotion when your feelings are hurt or when you stub your toe in the middle of the night. So strong are these emotions, that sometimes we are motivated to say and do things that we shouldn't. Your emotions are motivators. Unholy emotions motivate you in the direction of destruction in the plan of God. By default, then, most holy emotions motivate you towards the direction of success in the plan of God.

Paul's preaching was so full of utterance from the Spirit, that it would reach into the hearts of men and stir up their most holy emotions and motivate them towards the will of God – thus persuading them. This took place during the preaching of the gospel and the demonstration of the power of God. This is the method that Paul used to go into pagan, humanistic, and in some cases agnostic cultures and bring people into the kingdom of God.

An Effectual Door

1 Corinthians 16:9
For a great door and effectual is opened unto me, and there are many adversaries.

Paul says that there is a door in front of him, but there are adversaries present. When the Bible speaks of doors, it can mean a myriad of things. Doors can refer to people (John 10:9), the hearts of men (Revelation 3:20), an entry to a sheepfold (John 10:2), or the mouth (Psalms 141:3) – just to name a few. But in this passage of scripture, Paul is describing a door of opportunity to preach the gospel to a region. It is a large and effectual door. This implies that should Paul walk through the door, his ministry will have a huge effect on the people in that region.

Another thing to note in this scripture is that the door isn't just present; it's open. In other words, access has been granted to enter the door. But just because the door is open doesn't mean that entrance into the door is guaranteed. We know this because Paul brought attention to the adversaries that are present at the door.

Ministries go through seasons. Pastors and their churches will enter seasons through doors similar to what Paul talked about. Opportunities for expansion and increase will present themselves but there are adversaries at the door. Adversaries can present themselves internally or externally. Adversaries are forms of opposition that the enemy uses to slow the progression of the gospel in a region or stop it all together.

Sometimes this manifests as disputes among church members (music department, church board, pastoral staff, etc.). All of these things are designed to distract the pastor and the church from the effectual door that's open before them. Financial concerns and persecution from the community can be used as tools of discouragement to keep the ministry from moving forward.

But one thing I like to do is write the word *defeated* everywhere I see the devil or his devices mentioned in the word. So with this in mind, the scripture would read like this:

For a great door and effectual is opened unto me, and there are many **defeated** adversaries.

It's important that we know that Jesus has already spoiled principalities and powers (Colossians 2:10). The devil is a defeated devil with defeated devices. We have no reason to be afraid or be intimidated by his tactics. The remedy for any of his attacks is to be skillful in prayer and our authority as believers. The local church can be skillful in prayer by knowing how to pray the right prayer to cause the pastor and the vision to excel and thrive in the community.

Prayer antics like warring tongues and tearing down strongholds aren't spelled out in the New Testament. Being militant in prayer doesn't always equate results if it fosters a defeated mindset. Most people who subscribe to warring tongues, are not aware of the fact that the Bible says when you speak in tongues, you're speaking to God – not the devil (1 Corinthians 14:2). You are speaking in the tongues of men and angels (1 Corinthians 13:1), but nowhere in the New Testament are we instructed to address the devil in other tongues. Warring tongues is contrary to the Bible doctrines laid out in the Word concerning prayer. When we engage in such practices, it opens the door to further deception that leads to diminished results in prayer.

We aren't fighting to get the victory. We already have the victory by virtue of our identity in Christ. When we engage in spiritual warfare, we enforce the victory that Jesus has made available to us. The tricky thing about enforcing the victory of Christ is that we can't enforce victory in areas that we don't have authority. We have authority in our own lives, but we can't exert our authority over someone else's life. People have a free will and no matter how anointed and victorious we are, we can't usurp that.

Prayer will not break the stronghold in an individual's mind; only the entrance of the Word will do that. But what we can do is pray for strong utterance to invade their hearts and outrun the deception in their minds. We can pray that they will be able to hear the Word clearly and accurately, unhindered by satanic forces. Prayer was not designed to override an individual's free will.

When we follow the pattern that Jesus and Paul laid out for us and pray for laborers to be sent into unreached regions and pray for utterance, we will see the gospel preached and demonstrated in our cities. God is faithful to answer prayers that coincide with His plan. But He is not obligated to answer prayers that are merely the expression of religious brainwashing and deception. The best way to be led by the Spirit in prayer is to be led by the Word. Always return to the Word and expose prayer assignments and strategies to New Testament doctrine; make the necessary corrections and then proceed watchfully.

Praying for Utterance

Ephesians 6:18-19
Praying always with all prayer and supplication in the Spirit, being watchful to this end with all perseverance and supplication for all saints – and for me, that utterance may be given to me, that I may open my mouth boldly to make known the mystery of the gospel.

What is *utterance*? It is not merely speaking. When the Bible speaks of utterance, it's talking about a revelation of the gospel that will bring liberty to the listener. Utterance will bring the answers to the problems that plague a region. When a minister stands up with utterance, they have the proclamation of the gospel and the demonstration of the gospel. People need both.

Without the demonstration of the gospel, Christianity is nothing more than a philosophy, or a good idea. But when pastors can preach and demonstrate the gospel of Jesus Christ, regions can experience the love of God in unlimited proportions as the power of the God flows through the local church and into the communities. But the local church will never step into that flow with utterance. Prayer unlocks utterance. This is why Paul aggressively asked for the churches to pray that he would have it.

Paul didn't just want to preach the gospel; he desired that God would open his mouth and enable him to speak boldly. There is a difference between your pastor opening his mouth and God opening your pastor's mouth. When we think about the story of Balaam and his donkey, we can see what happens when the Lord grants utterance to an individual.

Balaam was on a journey to prophesy against Israel. While traveling, the donkey that he was riding became aware of an angel that was sent to oppose his travel plans. So the donkey became obstinate and began to draw back. This happened repeatedly, so Balaam beat the donkey. Numbers 22:28 says, "Then the Lord opened the mouth of the donkey, and she said to Balaam, 'What have I done to you, that you have struck me these three times.'"

Did you catch that? The Lord opened the mouth of a donkey and gave the donkey the ability to speak; not just to other donkeys but to a human being. God gave him the ability to speak and to be understood by a human being. This is the difference between just talking and utterance. I'm pretty sure that the donkey had opened its own mouth many times that day. The donkey probably made donkey noises and ate or drank throughout the day. There was nothing supernatural happening with that donkey until the Lord opened his mouth.

The same things happen in the local church. There is nothing supernatural that will happen with your pastor until the Lord opens their mouth. You may have a good church service, with good music, and good people. But you'll never bring about a substantial change being comfortable with mediocre church life. Mediocre church life is content with not reaching the unchurched. It's content with not seeing people healed and filled with the Spirit on a consistent basis.

Therefore there isn't a cry for utterance. So Paul told the people in the churches, "Pray for me! Pray that I would have utterance and be able to speak this mystery into the lives of the people God is sending me to." When a pastor has utterance, God supernaturally fills their spirit and their mouth with the answers that will bring deliverance to the people in the pews. Utterance makes the Word palatable and applicable.

Prayer for Boldness

Paul wanted them to pray for utterance, but then he also said pray for boldness. Boldness is more than having a demonstrative demeanor or attitude. When we think of boldness, many times we think of someone who is outspoken or pushy. But when the Bible speaks of boldness, it paints a very different picture. Look at how the people in the book of Acts prayed for boldness.

Acts 4:29-31
Now, Lord, look on their threats, and grant to Your servants that with all boldness they may speak Your Word, by stretching out Your hand to heal, and that signs and wonders may be done through the name of Your holy Servant Jesus. And when they had prayed, the place where they were assembled together was shaken; and they were all filled with the Holy Spirit, and they spoke the word of God with boldness.

They didn't ask for more volume in the preaching. They didn't ask for God to change their demeanor while ministering. They asked for the type of boldness that produced something more than eloquent speech. What they were asking for was a demonstration of the Spirit and power of God (1 Corinthians 2:4). "Grant unto your servants that with all boldness they may speak your word, by…" They asked God to grant them boldness by doing something. The boldness to preach was going to spring up because of something that God would do.

"Grant…boldness…by stretching forth your hand to heal and that signs and wonders may be done through the name of Your holy Servant Jesus." They asked for the demonstration of the gospel that they were preaching. It is the demonstration of the gospel that brings boldness to the proclamation of the gospel. You can be a little more confident in what you preach when you can demonstrate it. They didn't just want a good message they wanted bold utterance.

When bold utterance hits a region it goes to every front: social, financial and political. Everything is affected by the utterance of the Spirit. Utterance is a prophetic word that goes forth out of the mouth of the pastor and roots out corruption and doubt. Then it plants hope and faith for a better future in the hearts of the hearer. It brings a sense of accountability to the plan of God for the believer.

Bold utterance will snatch an addict out of their addiction and bring them face to face with the glorious light of the gospel. Bold utterance will bring a cure for AIDS to someone who is on their deathbed. It can make cancer and other diseases melt away because the gospel is the power of God unto salvation - spirit, soul and body (Romans 1:17).

This is what Paul admonished the churches to pray for him and it is a lesson for us to learn. Pray fervently for utterance. When you pray for utterance, God will release a prophetic word through your pastor that can alter the atmosphere of your church, your home and your region. I cannot stress the importance of praying for utterance.

It can pave the way for a family on welfare to come out of the ghetto. Utterance can bring a solution to a crime-ridden city where gangs are taking over neighborhoods inch by inch. The local church can put a stop to the corruption in their local government when bold utterance is flowing from their pulpits.

How is this possible? Utterance will develop Bible based beliefs in the hearers. These Bible based beliefs will begin to govern what they think, say and do and thus have an immediate effect on their voting and decision making. This is how we change a region.

I want to challenge you to partner with your pastor in prayer. Don't just go to church, hear the Word, pay your tithe and leave. Invest your heart into the vision by allowing it to alter your praying. As you pray for your pastor and the vision that God has given them, it will expand your capacity to receive more prayer assignments for them. Partner with them in prayer, and as you do, you will become more useful to God's plan for that church.

Review Questions

A. What does the pastor's ministry entail?
B. What was Paul's ministry philosophy?
C. Why is it important to pray for utterance and boldness?

Tweetable Moments

- Prayer initiates a chain of events that can lead to an invasion of God's

power in a region. @MarcusTankard #PrayerSecrets
- 🐦 People have a free will and no matter how anointed and victorious we are, we can't usurp that.
@MarcusTankard #Prayer Secrets
- 🐦 Bold utterance can bring a flow of solutions to a region
@MarcusTankard #PrayerSecrets

9 PRAISE AND WORSHIP

Psalms 76:1
In Judah God is known; His name is great in Israel.

The name Judah literally means *praise*. When we praise God, we see His character on display in a way that we don't experience anywhere else. Praise brings a manifestation of Him that we don't see any other way. I believe this is so because praise is the highest expression of faith. When you move into praise and worship, it is an indication that your heart has fully received the answer to your request. Because you believe that you have received, you stop asking and you enter into thanksgiving for what you believe God is going to do. Faith is what pleases God (Hebrews 11:6), so it is of no surprise that God is pleased to be the recipient of heartfelt praise and worship.

Praise and Worship Bring Total Victory

2 Chronicles 20:22-25
When the King Jehoshaphat and his people were faced with three armies, the king called a time of prayer. Out of that place of prayer they received a word that assured them that they would be victorious. When you really believe that God is going to do what he said, you will position yourself to receive the manifestation. This is exactly what Jehoshaphat did. Being fully persuaded of what God said, Jehoshaphat led the people into battle and placed the singers out front.

Now when they began to sing and to praise, the Lord set ambushes against the people of Ammon, Moab, and Mount Sier, who had come against Judah; and they were defeated. For the people of Ammon and Moab stood against the inhabitant of Mount Seir to utterly kill and destroy them. And when they had made an end of the inhabitants of Seir, they helped to destroy one another. So when Judah came to a place overlooking the wilderness, they looked toward the multitude; and there were their dead bodies, fallen on the earth. No one had escaped. When Jehoshaphat and his people came to take away their spoil, they found among them an abundance of valuables on the dead bodies, and precious jewelry, which they stripped off for themselves, more than they could carry away; and they were three days gathering the spoil because there was so much.

As the singers praised God, the Holy Ghost started moving on their behalf.

God heard their prayer, but the manifestation of victory didn't begin until they acted on their faith and praise began to flow. What would have happened if the singers and the army had stayed in bed that morning? I cannot stress the importance of getting in position to receive what God has said. Just because God has said something doesn't ensure that you will receive what was said. It's like playing catch: just because someone throws a ball doesn't mean that you will be the one to catch it. Only the person who gets in position will catch the ball. The same thing applies to faith: only the person in position will catch or receive a manifestation.

Praise positions you to receive from God. With hands lifted up and a mouth full of heartfelt words of adoration and thanksgiving, you are in the flow of the power of God. This works when your praise is an expression of your confidence towards God. Don't reduce this to an intellectual exercise where you thrust meaningless words into the atmosphere but you doubt inwardly. Faith is of the heart and therefore praise is to flow from your heart. When praise comes from the faith in your heart, it launches you into another the dimension of faith. It moves you from believing to receiving.

When the singers started to praise God, the scriptures say the Lord set ambushes against the three armies that were against Israel. God caused confusion to break out among the ranks of the armies and they destroyed themselves. That's an amazing feat, but its not total victory. You haven't received total victory until you recover spoils. A victory isn't a real victory unless you win something. Otherwise there would be no incentive to winning. When you keep your faith connected to God with a continuous flow of praise on your lips, He will lead you from victory to victory. That doesn't mean you won't have to fight; no one has ever heard of an effortless victory. You will have to be fervent with your faith, confession, and your praise. But on the other side of it are the spoils of war.

It says that it took the people three days to collect the spoils of war. God brought a whole nation into complete victory because of a series of faith acts. The highest expression of faith is your praise. Allow the praises of God to usher you into His presence where there is a flow of total victory.

Praise Brings a Flow of Peace

Philippians 4:6 Be anxious for nothing, but in everything by prayer and supplication with thanksgiving, let your requests be made known to God; and the peace of God, which surpasses all understanding, will guard your hearts and minds through Christ Jesus.

God has designed prayer, praise and peace to flow together. You should end every prayer time with a few moments of praise and worship. You haven't entered into the fullness of faith until you praise God. Praise God for hearing you because you know if he heard you, then you have the answer to your petition (1 John 5:14). Praise Him for what He spoke on the inside of your heart as you were praying. Sometimes it's hard to hear from God on certain matters because we don't value His voice enough to thank Him when He speaks. Thank Him for living in you and leading you into all truth. As you thank God for who He is and what He has already done for you, it moves your attention off the problem and onto Him. As He is the central theme of your focus, there is a flow of peace from His heart to yours.

Peace is one of the fruits of the Spirit and praise is one way to cultivate it. When you worship the prince of peace, you receive an impartation of His peace that can usher you through any situation you come up against. How do you tap into this peace? By offering prayers with praise. This is one of the main reasons that people leave prayer just as depressed as they were before they started praying. No matter how many scriptures you know, your faith will never stand the test of time until you step into the flow of peace. But the peace of God is beyond your reach if praise is not coming out of your heart.

Praise Stills the Avenger

Psalm 8:2 KJV Out of the mouth of babes and sucklings hast thou ordained strength because of thin enemies, that thou mightiest still the enemy and the avenger.

Some translations translate the word *strength* as praise. When you boast of the goodness and the might of God, it silences the devil. The enemy will try to pull you into agreement with him by introducing thoughts of doubt and fear. He has designed the bombardment of anxiety and discouragement to drive you out of faith and into unbelief; butut praise will put your faith in position to outrun any device the devil is trying to work in your mind. When you have stocked your heart full of the Word of God, it becomes an arsenal for prayer and praise. All you have to do is pull on what you know about God and His word . Then insert those scriptures into praise toward God. As you speak those things out of your mouth, you are not only bringing God glory, you are also encouraging yourself and fortifying your faith. You'll find that as you are praising God, the enemy has stopped speaking. Praise will gag the enemy every time. But it must be fervent, sincere, and based on the Word.

I have used my praise to outrun pain and symptoms in my body. I recall a time in my life when I was receiving my healing concerning some digestive issues. When the enemy would try to bring lying symptoms back into my body, it was like a flood of despair would flood my mind. At times I would get so overwhelmed with these thoughts that my physical strength would leave me. I did what I'm teaching you to do right now.

As I began to praise God, the Holy Spirit would bring healing scriptures that assured my healing was forever settled. These scriptures energized my faith and fueled my praise. Before I knew it, strength had invaded my being and doubt had been washed out of my mind. The river of God's presence coupled with renewing elements of His word, washed over my whole being and brought me back into complete harmony with God – spirit, soul and body.

You never have to sit and listen to the devil talk. You can cut off the flow of his conversation by opening your mouth and speaking the Word in praise and thanksgiving towards God. When the enemy comes in like a flood, allow the Spirit of God to raise up a standard with your faith filled praise (Isaiah 59:19). Praise and worship can take you to a place in God that your mind and emotions can't find, but they will be affected by. Your whole being feels the effects of His presence. But you have to bring whole self into the arena of faith with your words. When you praise and worship God, you step out of the realm of thoughts (where the devil is fighting you) and you step into the realm of the Spirit where your victory is forever settled. Silence your adversary and strengthen yourself by praising God.

Praise Holds You in Faith

Colossians 4:2

Continue in prayer, and watch in the same with thanksgiving.

When you have made your petition and your time of prayer has come to a close, you can remind God of what you have prayed about. You can do this from a place of faith and not panic. Watching with thanksgiving does this. Put God in remembrance of His word and remind Him that you are expecting Him to do what He said (Isaiah 43:26). This is the persistence of faith.

Some people have reduced prayer to a session with Santa Claus. You just sit in His lap, drop of your list and never mention it again. But that's not how faith works. Paul said to "continue in prayer and watch…" You must continue in both. When you stop continuing you have stopped the flow of faith. This is why Kenneth E. Hagin would exhort people receiving their healing to keep the switch of faith turned on. What does that mean? It means to keep a flow of words flowing in the direction of your miracle. Never stop confessing, praying and praising until you see the full manifestation of what you believe for.

Praise has an ability to refresh your vision. When you get into praise and worship, it allows the Holy Spirit to keep the fire burning in your heart concerning your request. The enemy has a tendency to strategically plant people and situations in your path to contaminate your faith. He will make sure that someone shares his or her experience with you in an effort to discourage you. If you're believing God for cancer to be healed, the devil will make sure that you notice every billboard, magazine ad, social media post and commercial hospice care. He's trying to replace the vision of life and healing with death and despair. You can safeguard yourself from those attacks by surrounding yourself with praise and thanksgiving.

I encourage people who are in need of healing to keep praise and worship playing in their home at all times. It doesn't have to play loudly all the time. You can turn it down very low at night and then turn it up as you want to hear it. But take control of the atmosphere of your home by creating one of praise and worship. An atmosphere of praise and worship is welcoming to the healer, Jesus Christ. If you'll keep drinking of His presence in praise and worship, His presence will make you whole. But you have to keep drinking. You have to keep the switch of faith turned on. You must continue in prayer and watch in the same with thanksgiving.

Praise Versus Worship

Someone once asked me, "What's the difference between praise and worship?" That is a complicated question. And I don't attempt to do an extensive teaching on it in this book because our focus is on prayer as a whole. Praise and worship are kind of like the gifts of the Spirit in the sense that they overlap in manifestation. We only separate praise and worship to define them because they run together.

Praise is celebration, admiration and adoration on display through word and action. When you praise God, you are thanking him for what he has done, is doing or is going to do on your behalf. Praise is primarily based on God's performance in your life. Defeat has a look, but praise has a sound. There is no such thing as unexpressed praise just like there is no such thing as silent thanksgiving. When someone is thankful, it is expressed in word and/or deed. When we are thankful for what God has done or is doing in our lives, it is expressed in heartfelt words and actions that can be felt and experienced by us and witnessed and received by him.

Worship takes on a deeper internal dialogue that produces a more pronounced, intentional expression. Worship is three parts: honor, love and hunger. While praise changes your perspective, I believe that worship changes your posture. The change of posture comes because of something that happens in your heart. The Greek word for worship is *proskenuo*. It is a compound word: *pros* means to lie prostrate. It speaks of deep humility and honor towards an object of affection. Worship calls on us to recognize who God is and who we are not. Then we submit that before God as an offering knowing that in Him we live, we move and have our being.

When you couple these two dynamics together, they will bring you into the reality of God's presence. This is why it is a good thing to begin your prayer time with praise and worship. When you come into His presence, you become less aware of your problem and more aware of Him. Hebrews says that when you come to God, you must believe that he is a rewarder of those who diligently seek Him (Hebrews 11:6). That simply means that when you enter God's presence with faith, He rewards you with Himself. He becomes that which you need. Sometimes we don't need an answer to a request as much as we need healing in our emotions. Jesus is still the healer and He can manifest His healing power in an atmosphere of worship where faith is flowing. Maybe you don't need more money; the situation in your finances could be springing from a wisdom problem. Jesus has been made wisdom for us (1 Corinthians 1:30). You draw from the well of wisdom in Him while you are in His presence. All of this can take place before you utter one word of a request.

His presence tends to bring your problems into perspective in such a way, that many times you find your answer before you ask for anything. This is why we cannot allow ourselves to become slaves to rules and mechanics in prayer. We must remember that we are talking to a person – God. He is not a machine; he is a divine personality. When you respond to Him as such, it will keep your prayer times from becoming robotic and predictable. Praise and worship has a lot to do with maintaining the flow of reality in your prayer time. So make it an uncompromising part of your spiritual disciplines.

Lies Concerning Corporate Praise and Worship

1. "Everybody worships in their own way".

Not only is that unscriptural, it is illogical. In every religion there is an order or system of worship. If where there is no set outline of liturgical worship, there is still an expression of worship available. So to think that we can approach God anyway we want is an indication that lawlessness is having its way with us. We have to resist lascivious thinking that suggests that we have options where God has given concrete instructions. God has listed many ways in which we are to worship: lifting hands (134:2), thanksgiving (Psalms 100:1-5), exuberant and emotional praise (Psalms 149:3), shouting (Psalms 117:1), worship music (psalms 150), kneeling (Psalms 95:6), and prophetic songs (Psalms 22:3; Ephesians 5:18-20).

I personally believe that singing a new song out of your heart is the highest expression of worship because of what it does. The new song is prophetic. God is a singer (Zephaniah 3:17). So when you sing to the Lord and then allow Him to sing back to you, you are writing words from His heart on the canvas of your heart. I think this is one of the reasons Paul told us to desire to prophesy (1 Corinthians 14:39). It was not just so we could prophesy to other people as much as it was so we could add a God.

Prophecy brings a sense of awe and reality of God. There is something supernatural that takes place when we release heavenly melodies from heaven. It breaks strongholds of pride while releasing the life and nature of God over our lives.

2. "People are watching me."

Maybe they are watching; but then again, maybe not. Some people come to church so self-conscious that they can't worship. Others come to church and are people conscious. Then there are still others that come to church and you just thank God that they are conscious. As a worship leader you wonder if they dropped their bodies in the seat and went back to the house. All these things are designed to keep us from being God-conscious. God inhabits the praises of His people – publically and privately. When He inhabits a space, He brings the expression of His person with Him. So whatever you need Him to be, He brings that expression with Him to accommodate your faith. But if you have allowed yourself, the devil or the presence of other people to highjack your worship, you don't step into the flow of the Spirit for that moment. You want the flow of the Spirit because there are answers for your life in that flow. I have witnessed the lack of praise and worship stifle the move of the Spirit in worship services. Why? It's because corporate praise is designed to bring everyone into a collective sound of worship for a corporate experience of God's presence and power. When you shut off the supply of worship, you keep people away from the one who has their answer, Jesus.

3. "Worship is for immature, weak-minded Christians."

Praise and worship is not something that you outgrow. There will never be a time when you can say, "Lord I know you're worthy of all praise but I've been praising you a long time and I think I've reached my quota for this season of my life. Because I know you're worthy, I don't have to tell you anymore because you know my heart." A thousand times no! We will be worshipping for eternity. And my thinking along these lines is that if worship doesn't satisfy you, its because you're not doing it right. You've got to get back to the Word and allow the person of Jesus Christ to thrill you again and draw you into thanksgiving and adoration. The Word of God reveals footprints that lead into His presence by inspiring affection, honor and devotion out of you. It paves the way into His presence. But you can't just read about God; you must press into experiencing him. Then and only then will you truly know the one that you serve intimately.

Secrets in His Presence

Psalms 25:14
The secret [of sweet, satisfying companionship] of the Lord have they who fear (revere and worship) Him, and He will show them His covenant and

reveal to them its [deep, inner] meaning.

The mysteries and secrets of God's plan for your life, the body of Christ, the nations and any number of things, are found within His presence. The success of any relationship is the fellowship that funds it. Without fellowship, there is no basis for a thriving relationship. It's not enough for you and God to have something in common. The blood of Jesus brings reconciliation between God and man, but it does not replace the need for conversation between God and man. The only way to transfer what is dear to you into the heart of God, and what is dear to God into your heart, is by way of meaningful conversation. Praise and worship paves the way to sweet and satisfying companionship with our father God.

From this place of intimacy, there is a flow of strategies for the plan of God. He will not only reveal to you the spirit of His covenant, but He will also make it personal for you. So that when you read the Bible, it's not just mere words that God said to someone else. Those words leap off the page with the life of the one who desires to bless you in ways you cannot comprehend. God will reveal to you the inner meaning of life and purpose for you, your ministry, your business and even your family. But that kind of commentary doesn't come from having a casual acquaintance with Him. It comes from developing an intimate relationship with Him over time. This type of relationship with God will satisfy your deepest longing. But it all begins with knowing how to conduct yourself in His presence. Praise and worship is the journey and the destination. Do it and do it well.

Review Questions

1. What is the connection between praise and faith?
2. How does worship differ from praise?
3. Why is corporate praise and worship important?

Tweetable Moments

- Praise positions you to receive from God. @MarcusTankard #PrayerSecrets
- Praise and worship is not something you outgrow. @MarcusTankard #Prayer Secrets
- The success of any relationship is the fellowship that funds it. @MarcusTankard #PrayerSecrets

10 INTERCESSION

There are certain buzzwords that are associated with prayer and prayer ministry. There is nothing wrong with buzz words, but if clarity and definition are not presented, people who are not skilled in prayer will never be able to catch on and flow with those who are more seasoned. One thing that I've found is that many people who use these buzzwords don't have a clue what they mean. So for the sake of bringing everyone on the same page and to keep from assuming that you know something you don't, I want to dedicate this lesson to the topic of intercession. I'm sure you've heard terms like intercessory prayer, intercessor, and intercession used before. But you may not be as well versed on these terms as you would like.

Let's be clear: intercession in its simplest form is not prayer. It is a concept. The term *intercessory prayer* is not even in the Bible; but the concept of intercession most certainly is in the Word from Genesis to Revelation. Intercession is to act or go between for the purposes of reconciliation.

Romans 8:34 KJV
Who is he that condemneth? It is Christ that died, yea rather, that is risen again, who is even at the right hand of God, who also maketh intercession for us.

Some have read this scripture and have assumed that because Christ is making intercession for us, that he is praying for us at the right hand of God. But that's not what this scripture is saying. Paul said that Christ not only died for us, but he "maketh intercession for us." What does that mean? It means that the sacrifice that Christ made for us in His death, burial and resurrection supplied eternal redemption for us all. There is no need for Him to be crucified, buried and resurrected again. His sacrifice is enough and His blood speaks eternally in the heavens while His presence at the right hand of God is the expression of a continual flow of intercession between you and God.

Hebrews 10:11-14 NKJV
And every priest stands ministering daily and offering repeatedly the same sacrifices which can never take sins away. But this man [Jesus], after He had offered one sacrifice for sins forever, sat down at the right hand of God, from that time waiting till His enemies are made His footstool. For by one offering he has perfected those who are being sanctified.

When you limit your definition of intercession to prayer, you reduce the intercessory ministry of Jesus Christ. Intercession is bigger than prayer. It is the act whereby reconciliation is brought to a person who is disconnected from God. Intercession is a work of mediation and representation. Jesus as the great intercessor mediated our case with God. He represented us to God and he represented God to us. His shed blood made a way to settle the case against us; for the wages of sin is death (Romans 6:23). And by this intercessory ministry, we have eternal redemption and an audience with God to pray.

Prayer and Intercession

What does the intercessory ministry of Jesus have to do with prayer? Everything! As Christians, we are partakers of the divine nature of Jesus Christ (2 Peter 1:4). Jesus invites us in intercessory ministry with Him as co-laborers (1 Corinthians 3:9). We don't have any delivering or saving power in and of ourselves. But because we have been made one with Jesus and are partakers of His nature, we are able to be an extension of His intercessory ministry by preaching the Word of reconciliation and faithfully praying for the lost.

. 2 Corinthians 5:17-21
Therefore, if anyone is in Christ, he is a new creation; old things have passed away; behold, all things have become new. Now all things are of God, who has reconciled us to Himself through Jesus Christ, and has given us the ministry of reconciliation, that is, that God was in Christ reconciling the world unto Himself, not imputing their trespasses against them, and has committed to us the word of reconciliation. Now then, we are ambassadors for Christ, as though God were pleading through us: we implore you on Christ's behalf, be reconciled to God. For He made Him who knew no sin to be sin for us, that we might become the righteousness of God in Him

God has committed us to the ministry of reconciliation. That includes sharing the word of reconciliation with those who have not been reconciled to God. Sinners do not know that Jesus has dealt with the sin and sinner problem. His blood not only washed them of their sin, it enabled them to experience a new existence. Old things have passed away and all things have become new. God is not holding their sins against them any more. He came to earth in a body (Jesus Christ), died and was resurrected in order to be reconciled to humanity. This is the word of reconciliation that we share with the world and it is an extension of Christ's intercessory ministry. When we preach the gospel, we become the vocal expression of His intercessory ministry because we testify to its reality and its effects.

When we answer the call to labor with Christ, we become ambassadors for Him. We are then charged with the task re-presenting Christ and His love to our generation. With word of reconciliation we act as a go between or mediator for God and man for the purpose of reconciliation. But we are not only invited to be ambassadors for Christ. Mediation and representation is a two way street. God desires that we stand in His presence with a posture of prayer for the lost in what we call intercessory prayer.

God is Looking for Intercessors

Ezekiel 22:30
The people of the land have used oppressions, committed robbery, and mistreated the poor and needy; and they wrongfully oppress the stranger. So I sought for a man among them who would make a wall, and stand in the gap before Me on behalf of the land, that I should not destroy it; but I found none. Therefore I have poured out My indignation on them; I have consumed them with the fire of My wrath; and I have recompensed their deeds on their own heads," says the Lord God.

God is actively looking for intercessors. What is an intercessor? An intercessor is an individual who makes himself or herself available to pray out plans and agendas that are in the heart of God. Availability is key to an intercessory; the more available an individual is, the more God can entrust them with things to pray about. The ministry of intercession is not given to a small number of believers. Everyone is called to pray. The sad reality is that there are few who give themselves to prayer and walk in a place where their heart is sensitive to receive prayer assignments from the Lord. God calls us all to come into His presence and receive grace and mercy for families, our churches, nation and ourselves. But few answer the call and remain consistent in the call.

When you see someone who is given to prayer, it seems like the presence of God follows them. As they pray it's as if power is in every syllable of their words. That happens because they have developed an acquaintance with God and His power. God hasn't given them a special ability to pray; they have simply cultivated their prayer life so they are familiar with how prayer works and how to administrate the power of God. This kind of lifestyle is available to anyone who will make themselves available to the Spirit of God – He's the one who transmits the assignments to our hearts.

Ezekiel lived during a time when the people who needed God's assistance the most were oppressed, robbed and mistreated. The judgment of God is simply the law of sowing and reaping in operation. Romans 6:23 says that the penalty of wrongdoing is death. It may not result in an immediate physical death, but there will be a penalty played out in some area – generally in the same area of the wrongdoing. The anger of the Lord was against the people who oppressed the poor. But in His mercy, God looked for a man or a woman to *stand in the gap* on the behalf of the people of the land.

What does it mean to *stand in the gap*? Many times we use these phrases in church, but don't have a clue what they mean. To *stand in the gap* is to intercede and pray. God was looking for someone to pray for the people of the land and in their praying stand in the gap or make up a wall between the people and the judgment their sin has brought on them. Remember that when you intercede, you serve as a mediator between God and the people. Sometimes that means that you pray and push judgment back so the individuals have time to repent. Judgment is simply a recompense for sin, but God loves people so much, he's not looking for an opportunity to judge people. This scripture didn't say that He was looking for some people to carry out judgment. It says He was looking for people to partner with Him in prayer to give sinners an opportunity to repent.

In the story of Sodom and Gomorrah, we see Abraham acting as an intercessor between God and the citizens of those cities. The sin of the people in those cities was so bad that it activated the judgment of God in their direction. God looked for a man to stand in the gap and He found Abraham. Many times people teach this story wrong because they think the main theme of the scripture is God's intolerance of sin. The message of the story is that God would have saved the entire city if there had been ten righteous people in the city.

But how did God arrive at the conclusion to save the city for ten righteous people? God and Abraham had a series of conversations about Sodom and Gomorrah. The Bible says "Come let us reason together," (Isaiah 1:18). When Abraham talked with God about those cities, he asked probing questions about the fate of the citizens. Back and forth he and God went as they discussed righteous people of the city and the fate of the sinners. This is a picture of our prayer times are to be like when are interceding for people. Persistence in intercessory prayer will give people an opportunity to see the error of their ways and get things right with God.

Intercessions and Supplications

1 Timothy 2:1
Therefore I exhort first of all that supplications, prayers, intercessions, and giving of thanks be made for all men…

Paul calls for supplications, prayers, intercessions and giving of thanks be made for all men. This is the Holy Spirit appealing to us through the apostle to enter the ministry of intercessory prayer. The prayer assignment in this scripture is not just for our unsaved family members, our pastors, or local politicians. We are to be praying for all men. In other words, every man is in need of prayer. Believers have access to the supply of heaven, so we should not be discriminatory with our supplications, prayers, intercessions and giving of thanks.

There are two words here in the scripture that can help us bring greater definition to the ministry of intercessory prayer: supplications and intercessions. There is a difference between the two. We know that prayer is making a request and to give thanks for an individual is simply to verbally be grateful to God for an individual's existence (life, health, ministry, job etc.). Intercession has been the focal point of this lesson, but what about supplication? What is it?

Ephesians 6:18
Praying always withal prayer and supplication in the Spirit, being watchful to this end with all perseverance and supplication for all saints...

Supplication is defined as passionate entreaty to God. What's the difference between intercessions and supplications? Notice in this scripture in Ephesians that it says that supplication is to be made for all saints. It doesn't say all men, but it does say all saints. So when we compare scripture with scripture, intercession is made for a sinner or one in danger of impending judgment. But supplications are made for saints. This makes sense when you realize that a Christian doesn't need someone to stand in the gap for them; they already have an audience with God. If anything, they need to learn how to exercise their own faith and get a revelation of who they are in Christ and His love for them. The sinner needs an intercessor to pray that the love and grace of God will reach them before the consequences of their actions catch up with them.

Strategies in Prayer for the Lost

Many Christians are ineffective in praying for the lost because they don't pray in accordance with the scriptures. Some people pray, "Lord save them. Save them Lord Jesus." The reality is that Jesus has already saved the world. God gave His son, and His son gave His life. The sacrifice that Jesus made was once and for all. To pray for God to save them, would be to ask for God to reenact the plan of salvation for one sinner. The sacrifice that he made was good for the totality of all humanity. So our prayer should not be that God save them. Their salvation is settled, they just need to receive the salvation that has been provided. Before an individual can receive salvation, they must hear the gospel message. This is where the bulk of our praying needs to be.

Matthew 9:36-38
But when He [Jesus] saw the multitudes, He was moved with compassion for them, because they were weary and scattered, like sheep having no shepherd. Then He said to His disciples, "The harvest truly is plentiful, but the laborers are few. Therefore pray the Lord of the harvest to send out laborers into His harvest."

Jesus being moved with compassion for the lost endeavored to impart that same love to His disciples. He says to them, "That harvest is truly plentiful, but the laborers are few. Therefore pray..." When you pray, you receive and impartation of God's love for people that you can't get any other way. Your affections follow your praying. So as you pray for the lost, your capacity to love them is expanded and you can receive even more extensive prayer assignments.

One of the greatest strategies to pray for the lost is in this scripture. Jesus instructed the disciples to pray for laborers to be sent into the harvest. Laborers are those who will carry the gospel message to those who need it. Sometimes in our zeal to get the gospel message out, we can make premature moves. Notice that Jesus didn't say, "The harvest is truly plentiful, but laborers are few. Therefore, go get busy! Tell everyone that you see that I'm here to save." That's not what Jesus said, but it's what many of us do.

We should have a zeal for the lost and a desire to win souls. But Jesus instructed us how to channel our energies when he said, "pray the Lord of the harvest to send out laborers into His harvest." Prayer is an organizing mechanism in the hand of God for laborers to be sent into the harvest strategically and accurately. God knows who will be the most effective in sharing the gospel message with an individual, people group or nation. We can endeavor to go in our own strength, but God will bless our endeavors as much as He can. If we really want to see people saved, we should submit to God's design for reaching the lost. He says pray and allow God to send.

1 Corinthians 3:6-9
I planted, Apollos watered, but God gave the increase. So then neither he who plants is anything, nor he who waters, but God who gives the increase. Now he who plants and he who waters are one, and each one will receive his own reward according to his own labor. For we are God's fellow workers; you are God's field, you are God's building.

Paul reveals the strategy that God uses to get the gospel to the lost. As we pray, God sends laborers who will sow the seed and water the seed. It is important to note that the person who sows the seed may not be the person who waters the seed. The person who sows, water and prayers may be three different people. But when everyone works together and does their part, God will get the increase. This should be a reminder that we are laborers with God in reaching the lost. God knows what method will be the most effective. The important thing is that when He calls on us to pray, that we are obedient to that command because the gospel agenda is set in motion when we pray.

Jesus said to pray that God would send laborers into the harvest. But the word *send* doesn't seem to capture the essence of what Jesus was trying to convey. A word study on the word *send* in this scripture reveals that it means to cast out, to command, to expel, or to draw out with force. As a missionary, I can tell you that these words fully describe the dynamic of being sent out into the harvest. There are so many things that take place in order for one person to hear the gospel.

In many cases, the laborer will have to leave their home, church and even nation to go across the world to preach the gospel to an unreached village. Other times, a laborer may have to stay at work late because their heart is leading them to share the gospel with a janitor in the workplace. There are different types of laborers for different types of people. Prayer will organize the lives of the laborer and the sinner to collide so the gospel message can flow and they can know Jesus Christ.

Sometimes it will take an individual hearing the gospel more than one time. Paul said, that one will sow the seed and another would water the seed. So the person who shares the gospel message may not be the person who leads the sinner in the prayer of salvation. That person may need to hear the message over and over again before their heart is open to receive. This speaks to the importance of persistent prayer on their behalf. We can't allow ourselves to be satisfied with praying for the lost when we feel like it or when *we* deem it necessary. If there is to be a constant flow of laborers into the harvest fields, then there must be a continual flow of prayers to send them.

2 Corinthians 4:3-4
But even if our gospel is veiled, it is veiled to those who are perishing, whose minds the god of this age has blinded, who do not believe, lest the light of the gospel of the glory of Christ, who is the image of God, should shine on them.

Satan is the god of this world. And he uses his influence to blind the minds of those who do not believe. He does this by filling their heads with ideologies and philosophies that deny the existence of God, promote a low self esteem and countless other thinking patterns that block the light of the gospel from setting them free. Our prayer should be that God will not only send laborers, but that these laborers would have such powerful utterance to share the gospel that the power of their words would dismantle and unravel every thought that exalts itself against the knowledge of God. We must pray that their words be full of demonstration and power (1 Corinthians 2:4). When there is a proclamation and a demonstration of the gospel, the light of Christ can flood their hearts and bring them to a place where they can make a rationale decision about their salvation. The goal is for them to experience the gospel message unhindered by any satanic influence. Intercession can make that possible.

Strategies in Prayer for Believers

Ephesians 1:15-19
Therefore I also, after I heard of your faith in the Lord Jesus and your love for all the saints, do no not cease to give thanks for you, making mention of you in my prayer: that the God of our Lord Jesus Christ, , the Father of glory, may give to you the spirit of wisdom and revelation in the knowledge of Him. The eyes of your understanding being enlightened; that you may know what is the hope of His calling, what are the

riches of the glory of His inheritance in the saints, and what is the exceeding greatness of His power toward us who believe, according to the working of His power.

In letters that Paul wrote to His churches, we are able to see what he prayed concerning the members of the churches. These prayers give us a clue into what is appropriate to pray over believers everywhere. The best way to be led by the Spirit is to be led by the word. These prayers will put us in position for the Holy Spirit to lead us into utterance and revelation in prayer.

Paul said they never ceased to pray that they would have the spirit of wisdom and revelation in the knowledge of God. Wisdom and revelation in the knowledge of God should be the foundation of everything that we do. Our ministries, businesses, relationships and every earthly endeavor should spring from a revelation of our Father God. When we have the spirit of wisdom and revelation, it will unlock a level of intimacy with God that we haven't experienced before. When you see who God is and how much He loves you, it will reveal another aspect of your identity. You can clearly see who He's made you to be.

So many believers are searching for satisfaction in careers, relationships or hobbies. But there is a void on the inside of you that cannot be filled with anything but God. There is definition to your existence that you won't get anywhere else. God is your creator and He knows what He's created you to do. The spirit of wisdom and revelation unlocks this mystery and brings you into the knowledge of the calling of God on your life.

When you pray this prayer over believers, the spirit of wisdom and revelation brings them into an awareness of their spiritual inheritance they haven't received yet. People struggle to receive promises from God because they are not aware of what has already been given to them. My wife and I hold healing crusades all over the world and we've found that most people struggle to be healed because they don't know that their healing is forever settled in heaven. Jesus was crucified over two thousand years ago and by His stripes we are healed (Isaiah 53:5). So people will pray and ask God to heal them not realizing He has already healed them! When we pray for the spirit of wisdom and revelation to manifest in the life of believers, their eyes are flooded with the light of God's Word concerning an aspect of their inheritance they haven't received.

Paul prayed that believers come to know "the exceeding greatness of His power." The flow of God's power is in accordance with our faith. But if we aren't conscious of the greatness of His power, we won't target our faith in that direction. The same power that got Jesus out of the grave is available to us. If that power will get Jesus out of the grave and provide eternal redemption for humanity, what will that power do for our family, finances, nation or church?

The power of God will work, but we must put our faith in God in order for the power to flow. Paul wanted us to know this power in an intimate way; not just experience it in times of crisis. I believe that God shares Paul's desire for us to experience the power of God. Jesus came to live in us so that we could be carriers of the power and glory of God into our communities.

Praying to this end will promote constructive spiritual growth and progress in the lives of believers. It will bring them into the knowledge of who they are in Christ and what God has placed them in the earth to do. Our prayers for other believers should help to pivot them in the direction of destiny. As the spirit of wisdom and revelation is manifested in their lives, what they learn about themselves and God's plan, they are launched into new orbits of their purpose and destiny.

Colossians 1:9-12
For this reason we also, since the day we heard it, do not cease to pray for you, and to ask that you may be filled with the knowledge of His will in all wisdom and spiritual understanding; that you may walk worthy of the Lord, fully pleasing Him, being fruitful in every good work and increasing in the knowledge of God; strengthened with all might, according to His glorious power, for all patience and longsuffering with joy; giving thanks to the Father who has qualified us to be partakers of the inheritance of the saints in the light.

Here is another prayer that Paul prayed over the believers. The first things he asks God for is that we would be filled with knowledge of the Lord's will in all wisdom and spiritual understanding. There are three key words here: knowledge, wisdom and understanding. Knowledge is knowing what to do; wisdom is knowing how to do it; and understanding reveals purpose by answer the question of *why*. These are indispensible gems to a believer because you can only please God to the degree that you know His will. When you are conscious of God's will for your life, everything else concerning you can come into alignment.

You will gain a clearer vision for your career, marriage and relationships when you know what the will of God is for your life. The will of God brings clear direction to the chaos of choices that world offers us. Paul didn't just want us to know God's will; he wanted us to be full of it. Being full of the knowledge, wisdom and understanding concerning the will of God doesn't leave room for discouragement, detours, and distractions. This gives your faith something to attach itself to so that now you can bring your entire life into symmetry with God's plan.

I used this prayer while in college. My first two years of college were a nightmare. I could hardly progress in my coursework because I was changing my major so much. When someone changes their major as much as I did, it is proof that they are not filled with the knowledge of the Lord's will. So I took this prayer and prayed it over and over again throughout the day. I think I did this for weeks. The more read this prayer to myself and before the Lord in prayer, the more I believed that God really had a unique plan for my life. One day I decided that I would carve some time out of my schedule to pray this pray and then pray in tongues for a while. It was the best decision that I ever made.

When I coupled this prayer with tongues, the spirit of wisdom and revelation flooded my heart. I began to get things in prayer concerning my purpose that I didn't walk into until ten years later. Some of the things I saw, I haven't manifested yet. I got so full of the God's plan for my life that it shifted my whole scholastic career. In one year, I transferred to another school to study world missions. And in less than three years I was on the mission field planting Bible schools in Europe.

These prayers are designed to launch you into new orbits of purpose. Imagine what these prayers will do for high school and college students in your church? What would happen if you began to pray these prayers over your children while they are toddlers? When you do that, you are building a future that is custom made for them. You are creating encounters with God where His purpose and plan can flood their hearts and pivot them in the direction of destiny. This is a whole lot easier than arguing with them about their friends or a college major.

I have prayed these prayers faithfully over my family members for years. I give glory to God that my siblings may not be perfect, but all of them have a grasp of God's plan for their lives. Praying the prayers that Paul prayed helped me to detach my emotions from the shock and embarrassment of their mistakes. These prayers helped me to engage my faith after I cast my care on God. When I did that, it opened my heart to receive wisdom on how to conduct myself concerning them. God would give me words seasoned with love and grace that would pierce their hearts and shift their paradigm. I wasn't in a position to receive what I needed from God concerning them when I was in worry and lashing out in anger over their mistakes. If I want to be a good big brother, I need to realize that I serve a big God. My God is more than enough for my family and me.

Parents can pray and watch God move in the life of your child. Sometimes God needs your prayers more than he needs your participation in discipline and instruction. Before you try to fuss and cuss them out, pray them out. Pray them through adolescence. Pray them through the college application process. Pray them through their collegiate career. Pray them through their singleness. Pray them through the turbulence of their relationships and finances.

Commit to fervent prayer in your parenting and you'll see a demonstration of the power of God in the lives of your children. People have said over and over again, "Oh I would do anything for my family." But will you use your faith and pray for them? If God told you to fast for twenty one days for your in laws, would you do it? We have been given prayer strategies that will work on any given situation if we will use them. Let the love of Christ motivate you in the direction of obedience to the Word to pray. No matter how well you know someone, God knows him or her better than you do. He knows exactly what will fix the situation. Don't try to figure it out on your own, just pray and watch God work and get the glory.

Prayer Strategies in Praying for Ministers

The success of any minister is directly tied to the supply that prayer brings in their direction. Ministers have a responsibility to stand before God in prayer concerning the people that they serve and the words that they preach. But the prayer burden doesn't rest exclusively on the minister. The hearers have a responsibility to pray for the minister and intercede for the people who will be under the influence of the message.

There are areas of ministry and results in ministry that the body of Christ will not (cannot) attain unless the church is praying. God never designed for ministry to be done independent of God's people. The church must shift our paradigm concerning ministry so that we can partner with men and women who are tasked with preaching. If we want to have the same results of the early church, then we must follow the pattern that was set for us. Paul was a man of faith, yet he asked for prayer constantly.

Ephesians 6:18-
Praying always with all prayer and supplication in the Spirit, being watchful to this end with all perseverance and supplication for all the saints and for me, that utterance may be given to me, that I may open my mouth boldly to make known the mystery of the gospel for which I am an ambassador in chains; that in it I may speak boldly, as I ought to speak.

Colossians 4:2
Continue earnestly in prayer, being vigilant in it with thanksgiving; meanwhile praying also for us, that God would open to us a door for the word, to speak the mystery of Christ, for which I am also in chains.

2 Thessalonians 3:1-2
Finally, brethren, pray for us, that the word for the Lord may run swiftly and be glorified, just as it is with you, and that we may be delivered from unreasonable and wicked men; for not all have faith.

When I read through Paul's requests for prayer, one thing stands out to me: Ministers rely on the assistance of God's people with God's plan. God birthed a vision in Paul's heart to minister to the Gentiles and then launched him into a trailblazing ministry that would set the standard for missionaries for years to come. The sending of Paul into ministry was bathed in prayer (Acts 13) so I would make sense that the ministry would also be maintained and progressed by prayer. His faith alone wouldn't do it. It would require the faith of God's people in prayer to fuel the progress Paul (and God) desired for ministry.

There are many ministers who are experiencing a vacancy in prayer for their ministry. This is why their ministries have stalled and are not breaking barriers with the same consistency they once did. It's easy to blame the minister and say, "You just need to pray more and get some strategies from God." But the reality is God is calling people with a spirit of prayer who can offer a supply towards that ministry that can thrust the ministers into new phases of ministry.

Occupying a place of prayer for a ministry is an assignment from the Holy Spirit. I believe that every member of the local church should occupy a place of prayer for their pastor(s) and the church. Prayer is what moves the plan of God forward. Faith-filled words that are thrust out into the spirit realm will frame, fashion and organize events and people to accommodate the will of God. Spirit-led prayer will nourish the mantle that rests on the minister and the ministry with wisdom, counsel, innovative ideas, witty strategies, finances and a host of other things. Whatever is needed is provided when there is a prayer supply made available.

Philippians 1:19
For I know that this will turn out for my deliverance through your prayer and the supply of the Spirit of Christ.

Prayer moves the supply of the Spirit. When you yield to the Spirit of God in prayer, He will inspire utterances (both in your known tongue and in other tongues) that will shift things in the direction of the plan of God. For example, Spirit-led prayer feeds the prophetic office. I remember a lady who recounted a story of how God used her in prayer this way. As she was praying she got an entire sermon in her spirit. She got the scriptures, points, introduction and conclusion all while praying. She said, "I thought the Lord was calling me to the ministry because I had this sermon burning on the inside of my spirit." The next week she attended a meeting being led by Kenneth E. Hagin. When he began preaching, his sermon was the exact sermon (scriptures, points etc.) that this lady had received in her prayer time. What happened? She prayed the sermon out and Brother Hagin preached it out.

This is the type of partnership that God desires for His ministers. He's looking for people who will partner with Him and His ministers in prayer to push the plan of God out and into the nations. The supply that prayer brings will create a platform for the minister to step out on for ministry. That platform is not one made of wood, metal or plastic. I'm talking about a spiritual platform that provides utterance and demonstrations of the Holy Spirit – a platform that will promote miracles, signs and wonders for everyone present in the meeting. Kenneth Copeland once said, "I know when my partners are not praying; I have weak utterance." Brother Copeland is a prophet of God and the weight of the prophetic word hinges on his partners' praying. Anyone can get up and preach a mini sermon and pray for a few sick people. But the nations require more than a speech and presentation. We must have words that pierce the hearts of men and manifestation of God's presence that leave a mark that cannot be erased.

How do we pray for ministers? What type of praying will promote a supernatural ministry? Prayers that are based on the will of God and led by the Spirit of God will produce the results we are after. Firstly, you'll want to pray for utterance. Utterance is the most important asset that a minister has in their arsenal because it carries the ingredient that God placed in them to bless the body. Whether they are a pastor, teacher, apostle, prophet or evangelist, the supply of their mantle is primarily passed by their words. So you'll want to make a concerted effort to pray specifically for utterance and demonstrations of the Spirit.

A demonstration of the Spirit is how God endorses the message that is preached. Want the gospel to be presented in full array? This happens when there's preaching and demonstration. Pray that the gifts of the Spirit would flow and confirm the word being preached. Pray that the people will not just come to church hungry for a move of God, but that they will come yielding to the movement of God in the service.

Beyond that, I generally suggest that you identify what the call is on the minister. This may take an orchestrated effort on your part. If you are not able to speak with the minister directly, you may have to talk to staff members or people who have been associated with the ministry longer than you. Tune your ear to listen for clues while the minister is preaching. You'll find glimpses of their calling in their preaching if you will set your heart to find them. Then, find out what is on their heart for this season. Is there a building program being promoted? Does the ministry want to expand their staff? What are the initiatives of the ministry that require prayer and intercession right now? The answers to these questions become your prayer assignments.

Romans 8:26
Likewise the Spirit also in our weaknesses. For we do not know what we should pray for as we ought, but the Spirit Himself makes intercession for us with groanings which cannot be uttered. Now He who searches the hearts knows what the mind of the Spirit is, because He makes intercession for the saints according to the will of God.

Once you have prayed out as far as you can in English, its time to pray in the

Spirit. This aspect of prayer is so important because it enables you to pray beyond the knowledge base of your mind. The Holy Spirit knows the plan much better than you do, so he can be trusted to inspire utterances in prayer that are laser sharp. He can be trusted to only give utterance to those things that will promote the interests of God concerning the plan.

There are sermons that are custom made for this present era. These messages will answer the needs of the social, financial and political arena of our nation. But these things have to be prayed out. This is why we are encouraged to pray for utterance. God will open doors for ministers and ministries to walk through, but utterance is what will enable us to reach our full potential in the rooms and spheres that God is sending us to.

There are stronger moves of the Holy Spirit that will flow out of places of prayer. Anointings for healing and miracles will flow freely when we corporately learn how to move with God. This begins when we stand before Him in prayer and release a prayer supply for our churches. The prayer supplies will furnish the meetings with what is needed for a move of God before the minister or the people show up. There is a greater intensity of the Spirit that God desires to see in our services. The Holy Spirit conveys the reality of God when we allow the gifts of the Spirit to reach their highest potential in our minds. Prayer and intercession paves the way for this to happen. So we can never underestimate what our prayers can do.

Review Questions

1. What is intercession?
2. How does intercessory prayer differ from supplication?
3. Why do we need to pray for ministers?

Tweetable Moments

- 🐦 Intercession literally means to stand in the place of another.
  @MarcusTankard #PrayerSecrets
- 🐦 Intercession is made for all men; supplication is made for all saints. Eph 6:19 1 Tim 2:1-5
  @MarcusTankard #Prayer Secrets
- 🐦 Ministers rely on the assistance of God's people with God's plan.
  @MarcusTankard #PrayerSecrets

11 PRAYER FOR YOUR GOVERNMENT

"The church as a whole [has] failed President Obama by praying partisan prayers and following conspiracy theories. The word of the Lord came concerning President Obama's coming. Once he was elected, the word came revealing my plan for his term and administration. While being too busy following the issues, conspiracy theories, and political rhetoric, my people did not pick up the prayer assignment from the prophetic word and aborted many of my plans for the last eight years of this nation. But I still have a plan. I have a plan for this land. And if you'll get in the Spirit you will hear it because you are near it. Yes the time is near for the church to change gears and move into what I've spoken for years. Where the governmental prophets arise and move into places of influence where the counsel of the Lord shall stand and flow into the hearts of the leaders of this nation. The strategies I have are not of might and power. But they are higher than the politics of man. So keep your praying spiritual and you'll see my hand move the hands of men. I will close doors and stop the adversaries of my plan in their track. And the gospel will have free course in this nation. It will move swiftly on the heels of those who will carry this message and power to the lost! So don't worry... continue to seek my face and employ my ways in the Spirit and you'll see what I've said come to pass."
Prophecy from July 17, 2015

In this prophecy, God specifically addresses the failure of the church with the Obama administration. But in addressing this, He also revealed three things that abort His plan for a presidential administration. When the Spirit of God reveals anything to us, it is for our profit, prosperity and progress (1 Corinthians 12:7; 2 Chronicles 20:20). The Holy Spirit never speaks just to hear Himself talk. He has purpose in His manifestation. So when we respond to him properly and not despise His movement (1 Thessalonians 5:20), we can experience success in every arena – including politics and government.

God's plan for a presidency is for His people to be able to live a life of godliness and peace so the gospel can reach the unchurched and unbelieving populace of a nation. The decisions that a commander in chief make directly and indirectly affect the influence of the gospel. I'm sure that these three things are not the only factors that inhibit God's plan for a presidential administration. But these are the particular things that He brought to my attention to as it refers to praying for our political leaders. And I want to use what He shared with me to inspire you to do the same.

Following the Issues

The first thing the Lord brought attention to was the habit of following the issues. Issues would refer to problems that affect our nation socially i.e., abortion, gun control, and immigration. What side of the issue you are on depends your political beliefs and philosophies. As a preacher it is my responsibility to preach the undiluted word of God for the purposes of developing Bible based beliefs in the listeners. As Bible based beliefs form, a system ethics and morality will begin to govern what we think, say and do. It is from this foundational belief system that our views of the issues should spring from. Because many Christians have various maturity levels, this makes for various opinions and paradigms concerning the issues.

Other things that can cause a difference of opinion are cultural beliefs. The historical treatment of a particular ethnic group or social conditioning can have a huge affect on how an individual processes the political process and their view of the issues. But according to 2 Corinthians 10:4, we have to expose every thought, tradition, philosophy or opinion on any given issue to the word of God. When we expose our thinking to the word of God, the light of the word will separate the light from the darkness – the truth from the deception. We cannot allow the demonically inclined culture to sedate us to the reality of sin and the consequences of it. If not, we will find ourselves promoting activities that are inspired by demons.

You cannot allow yourself to follow the issues more than you follow the Word and the Spirit. Your knowledge of the issues is not going to fuel your prayer life like the intelligence of the Spirit of God. When you allow an insatiable desire to be current on the issues remain in you, it can drown out the voice of God that's endeavoring to lead you into truth. You have to submit your opinion to the truth of the Word because the Holy Spirit is not going to help you pray your view of the issues. What if your view of the issue is wrong? What if your view of the issue is not God's highest or His best? You must submit your mind to the truth of the Word of God and submit your spirit to the leading of the Holy Spirit within you.

Following the issues will feed your intellect, but it won't feed your spirit. I'm not advocating that you put your head in a hole and dismiss any conversation or media story concerning the issues. These things are relevant to our society and we should have a working knowledge of these things. But we cannot be so immersed in issues that we become divisive, disagreeable and dismissive with the truth of God's word. Follow the issues, but keep your heart right so you can pray right.

Conspiracy Theories

I like a good conspiracy theory. In fact one of my favorite movie genres is crime drama. I enjoy connected time, events, and people in complex plots. Conspiracy theories in and of themselves are not wrong. But you cannot allow unnecessary attention to be given to conspiracy theories because it fosters a suspicious disposition. When President Obama was elected, theories of his birth certificate surfaced and dominated social media most of his presidency. As a nation, we couldn't really focus on bringing answers to the issues we were supposed to be following because we were distracted by conspiracy theories.

Do not say 'A conspiracy,' concerning all that this people call a conspiracy nor be afraid of their threats, nor be troubled. Isaiah 8:12 NKJV

God deliberately tells us not to call everything a conspiracy. Obviously we are to champion the truth and resist deception. But there is a big difference between championing the truth and allowing suspicion to have it's way with us. Suspicion is the fruit of fear and worry. It is a vicious cycle because the more you fear, the more you gravitate to conspiracy theories. The more complex the conspiracy theory the more you fear and search for more theories. It never stops. Sooner or later, you have to get delivered from fear and trust God. He didn't give you the spirit of fear. God gave you power, love and a sound mind. So a troubling heart is not a believing heart that's full of faith, power and love. When you have a sound mind, you have a disciplined mind that agrees with God; not a mind that goes on fishing expeditions for conspiracies.

…Charge some that they teach no other doctrine, nor give heed to fables and endless genealogies, which cause disputes rather than godly edification which is in faith. 1 Timothy 1:3-4

Paul instructed Timothy (a young pastor) to instruct the leaders in his church not to chase after strange doctrines, fables, and genealogies. Conspiracy theories would be inclusive in this list. Some preachers have allowed this stuff to captivate their minds and the minds of their parishioners. No one is praying because we are too amused by the next theory. And if there is any praying going on, it's laced in fear and not faith because we are praying based on the last theory we heard and not what God has said.

Conspiracy theories are divisive in nature. The disputes that arise from their discussion don't foster unity at all. Such things should not be tolerated among us. We should have enough love flowing through us that if any view on the issues or a given theory that promotes division can be put to the side for the sake of unity. A quest for truth should not lead any of us to demonize a group, political party or denomination.

Political Rhetoric

Some Christians have a messiah complex as it refers to political figures. This line of thinking believes that there is only politician that can be anointed for a given office. For anyone else to win the election, would be a detriment to the plan of God. So when "our guy" doesn't win, we tend to demonize the "other guy." If the politician isn't from our particular political party, we have a sour attitude for their entire presidency. This is not the love of God in operation. Sinners act that way – not people who know how to pray.

When we allow this line of thinking, we will combat any and everything a politician or political party does – whether it's right or wrong. We cannot allow ourselves to get so drunk on propaganda and rhetoric that w can't see straight. One of the tactics of war is promote propaganda. It's designed to inspire fear and promote a warped perception of reality. Some people have seen more propaganda than they have scriptures and then we wonder why our prayers don't make more power available for our governments.

Political rhetoric would have you to believe that recession is going to take over the world and you'll have to sell your kids for food by the end of the year. It will have you running around outside screaming, "The sky is falling! The sky is falling!" That's no way to live when serve a mighty God who is able to do exceedingly, abundantly above all you could ask or think (Ephesians 3:20). Curb your desire for rhetoric by desiring the sincere milk of the word of God. The milk of the word will promoted constructive spiritual progress and a balanced belief system. It will keep you out of doctrinal ditches and help you maintain and fruitful prayer life.

Activism

Following the issues, conspiracy theories, and political rhetoric left to themselves aren't wrong. But left unchecked can shipwreck your faith and derail your prayer life. Many times these things are the motivation for social and political activism. Let me give a word of caution here: nothing is wrong with activism. But activism doesn't not relieve you of your responsibility to do what God told you to do: pray. You can be an activist, but if you are not a pray-er, all your activism will have been in vain.

Activism is effective, but prayer is supernatural. Prayer will move the power of God over your nation. It will build up, tear down, overturn and rearrange policies, laws and people to accommodate the will of God. Don't limit your Christianity to activism. Sooner or later you're going to have to pray if you want to see the results that God has ordained you to see.

Sometimes we justify activism by saying that prayer isn't working. We make excuses and say, "I tried that prayer stuff. But it didn't work for me.

I don't think prayer is our problem." But the effectual fervent prayer of a righteous man will work (James 5:16). It's not that you tried prayer and it didn't work. Prayer tried you and you didn't work. Praying God's way will bring God's power. Some of us are more skilled in complaining than we are praying. So when we do pray for the government, we spend more time complaining about our leaders than we do actually praying God's plan. If you pray the problem, that's all you're going to have. Pray the solution and it will appear. We've got to use the tools that God has given us in His word in order to pray effectively. Pray God's plan and you will see god's plan.

A Lifestyle of Successful Praying

While you follow the issues, conspiracy theories, and political rhetoric, ask yourself this question: is this going to help me pray more effectively for my nation? That should be the litmus test for what you allow yourself to digest. You don't want propaganda to cloud your spiritual judgment.

Every seed will produce after its own kind. A word provokes a thought. Thoughts produce pictures. Pictures move thoughts from your head to your heart. Once the pictures are in your heart, they are painted on the canvas of your imagination and begin to feed strongholds of your mind. The words that spring from your heart that express your thoughts are merely the tip of a large iceberg in your heart. What you think, say and do are merely the expression of what you are yielding to inwardly and it is this internal dialogue that will either inhibit your praying or position you to pray supernaturally.

One way you can stay in the flow of Spirit led prayer is by developing a habit of exposing your thought life to God. The psalmist said in Psalm 19:14, "Let the words of my mouth and the meditation of my heart be acceptable in your sight." God already knows your thoughts. But we should desire to please Him – even in our hidden parts. I don't have to respond to a thought that God didn't author in me. So I endeavor to strengthen the inner dialogue that I have with God by talking to him or meditating on scriptures when I'm not talking to people or actively engaged in an activity that requires my reasoning.

By keeping my mind on God, it keeps my heart open to receive fresh utterance from heaven concerning anything that enters my life throughout the day. It helps to heighten my awareness of spiritual things so I'm not so easily carried into activities and conversations that don't deserve my attention. This is how I filter all of the stimuli that the media feeds me. I don't take my cues in prayer from what I see on the news or discover on social media.

The Holy Spirit feeds my spirit prayer assignments because I'm constantly watching in my heart for what he will say. If we take our cues from what is offered to us through media, debates, conspiracies, etc., we will find ourselves praying from a place of panic and not a place of power.

A lifestyle of prayer doesn't mean that you dismiss yourself from the responsibility to be informed about what is going on in our nation and world. But it does mean that you develop discernment on how you handle the information that is fed to you. We have to be serious enough about praying for our nation to actually do it. Talking about prayer and praying are two different things.

Paul, Politics and Prayer

1 Timothy 2:1
I exhort therefore, that first of all, supplications, prayers, intercessions, and giving of thanks, be made for all men: for kings, and for all that are in authority; that we may lead a quiet and peaceable life in all godliness and honesty. For this is good and acceptable in the sight of God our savior; who will have all men to be saved and come unto the knowledge of the truth.

Paul wrote this scripture during the reign of Nero – the worst political leader of that time. Here are some quick facts about Nero.

Nero Facts

1. He would capture Christians, dip them in oil and light them like candles.
2. He killed his own mother.
3. He killed his wife.
4. He sold positions in public office to the highest bidder.
5. He increased taxes and too money from the temples.

These are incredibly vile things for a man to do – let alone a politician. The thought of killing Christians in such a gruesome manner is hard to stomach. And to kill your own mother and wife violates everything that I believe not just as a Christian but also as a man. History says that he killed them due their disagreement with his conduct and ethics. The corruption surrounding his administration made him an incorrigible political leader because he sold position and influence through bribes, kickbacks and under the table deals.

But I find something very interesting as I study the letters of Paul. He never mentioned Nero in his writings – not once. Paul never mentioned him or bad mouthed him vicariously. There is something to be learned from Paul's lifestyle of prayer. By Paul's absence of acknowledging his disdain for Nero, he's saying don't complain – instead exercise your authority by praying.

Pray for All Men

Paul's instructions called for supplications, prayers, intercessions and giving of thanks to be made for all men. I remember the first time that I read this scripture and I thought to myself, "This poses a big problem – I don't even know all men. How am I going to pray for them?" It would be humanly impossible to pray for all seven billion people on the planet. I reasoned to myself that maybe the Holy Spirit would bring specific people to my heart to pray about at different times throughout the day. But that answer didn't seem to satisfy my heart.

The strategy to pray for all men is found in the same scripture that the instruction is given. The way that we pray for all men is by praying for kings and for all those who are in authority. When we pray for those who are in positions of authority to make decisions that influence all men, the supply of the Spirit can reach them and have an affect on their decision-making. Proverbs 21:1 says, "the king's heart is in the hand of the Lord, like the rivers of water; He turns it wherever He wishes." But cannot do that without the consent and intercession of His people (Psalms 115:16).

When we pray, we move the supply of heaven in the direction of our leaders. Heaven's supply manifests in the form of wisdom, counsel, divine relationships, health, wealth and a host of other things. Whatever is needed to get the job done, moves in the direction of the ones who need it when we pray. This calls for a consistent flow of faith and obedience. We must believe that God will honor His Word as we obey Him. This prayer strategy will enable us to live a quiet life in peace and godliness, thus making it easy for us to get the gospel to all men. God wouldn't tell us to do something that wouldn't work. But we must line our praying up with His strategy. Praying this way is the commandment of the Lord.

Our prayers will reach the highest seat of authority in the land. We have to meditate on these truths and allow them to have an effect on our self-image. Our prayers are not meaningless. God is not trying to waste our time with worthless spiritual disciplines. He asks us to pray because our prayers have an effect. When you realize the power of your words and the authority that you have been given in prayer, you will use it for the benefit of others.

Another thing to take note of is that God is pleased when we pray for our elected officials. Paul said that this prayer strategy is good and acceptable in the sight of God. So deductive reasoning tells me that my prayer life will never please God until this becomes a consistent priority. I can't wait until a presidential election and pray for officials that are going to be elected. God is calling for a consistent flow of the supply of heaven into the political arena because of the effect it has on the gospel getting to all men.

The Seat of Authority

Romans 13:1-3
Let every soul be subject to the higher powers. For there is no power but of God: the powers that be are ordained of

God. Whosoever therefore resisteth the power, resisteth the ordinance of God: and they that resist shall receive to themselves damnation.

The first thing we learn from this scripture is that God ordains authority. The position, or seat, of authority is ordained of God. God may not endorse the man or woman who sits in the seat, but the seat of authority itself is ordained of God. Whatever God ordains He anoints. To be anointed means to be empowered to function in a position or office. The seat of the presidency has anointing that rests on it that will enable the one who holds the seat to function properly. Proper function will make wisdom and counsel available for good decision-making that will promote peace and godliness in society as the gospel is preached to all men.

When an individual is elected or appointed to public office, they must choose to respond to the anointing that is on the seat of authority they possess. They have a choice: they can either submit to the anointing that is on the seat or they can submit to the demonic spirits that would love to influence them to make bad decisions. Many times, leaders are not conscious of the anointing that is on the seat or the demonic powers that desire to inspire them. God is not telling us to control the political leader. But your authority will control and hold back evil spirits that would try to control or influence them. We can bind those spirits from affecting our leaders so the influence of God can get in and prevail.

Every political leader is an expression of the one they are yielded to – God or the devil. Our responsibility as righteous men and women is to make power available to the one who is sitting in the seat of authority. Ultimately, it is up to them to choose to respond to good counsel and make wise decisions. This is why my prayer is not so much that God would allow Christians to get in office as much as it is that the people in office will respond to the power of God for the sake of the gospel.

Sadly, many times believers will dismiss themselves from getting involved in politics or legislative decisions because they are not actively involved in the decision making process. But just because you aren't actively involved with making a legislative decision doesn't mean that you don't have a responsibility to influence the decision with your authority as a believer. Your authority is released by your faith filled prayers. You have to send your words to prevail in the arenas that the devil would use to stop the progress of the gospel.

The Gospel Agenda

2 Thessalonians 3:1-3
Finally, brethren, pray for us, that the Word of the Lord may have free course, and be glorified, even as it is with you: and that we may be delivered from unreasonable and wicked men: for all men have not faith.

Paul encouraged the church at Thessalonica to pray for them using a strategy that gives more precision to how we can pray for our government and its affect on the gospel. The prayer is very simple: that the gospel will have free course and that we may be delivered from unreasonable and wicked men. Notice where the emphasis is: the gospel. Paul is not praying about issues, exposing conspiracies, or political rhetoric. Although God's light will expose and bring whatever is done in the dark into full of exposure. I believe that we should pray that the truth prevail, but I also believe that God has given us proven prayer strategies that will work if we will engage them.

What determines whether a political leader is unreasonable and wicked? The answer is very simple. Unreasonable and wicked leaders are individuals who limit the progression of the gospel by not responding to the anointing and godly wisdom that comes with their seat of authority. We must be delivered from wicked and unreasonable leaders – not necessarily unbelievers. God can use and unbeliever with a pliable heart that responds to good counsel and sound judgment. It's when leaders have set their hearts to rebel against the plan of God for a nation to hear the gospel that deliverance is required.

Men in authority have a direct effect on the gospel being preached. The gospel is the power of God unto salvation for our communities (Romans 1:17). Moral referendum and legislation will not heal our land unless the gospel invades the hearts of people and translates them out of darkness and into the kingdom of God. The revival our nation needs is not political – it's spiritual. We must have an awakening to God and to His plan. But it all starts with accurately praying out His plan for our leaders.

How Do We Pray

The best way to pray is to pray the Word. Extend your authority by speaking faith-filled words over the leaders of our nation. Pray that our leaders would respond to the power of God that accompanies their offices. Resist the temptation to only pray for Christian leaders and demonize people who don't share your political opinions and philosophies. God does not require Christian leaders to be in office before He moves in our governments. God has used wicked kings to promote His interests before and He's able to do it again (Nehemiah 2:1-9; Isaiah 45:1-4).

Take the highest route in prayer by praying prayers that are God inspired and God ordained. Love your leaders through your prayers. Paul said offer supplications, intercessions, prayers and giving of thanks. Can you say that you are thankful for your president, congressmen and senators? Maybe you're not thankful for their decisions and policies, but you can be thankful for their offices because God set the authorities in place. Speak what you want to see come out of that office. Declare that the counsel of God and sound judgment flow from those seats of authority. Decree that no weapon formed against them and their families will be able to prosper and that they will reach their full potential in the office(s) that they hold.

You can exercise your authority over the social, economic and political arenas of your nation by speaking faith filled words. Tell Satan to take his hands off of key leaders and declare that the influence of God is flooding every mountain of our culture. Pray that God would send laborers as representatives of His kingdom in to the high places that will take a flow of sound counsel for those in authority. All of these prayers are inspired from the prayer strategies given to us by Paul. The Holy Spirit can hook up with us when we pray this way.

After we have prayed out as far as we can in English, we can pray in other tongues. This is where the Holy Spirit will supply you with utterance (in tongues and English) that will allow you to be laser sharp in your praying. The Holy Spirit knows how to connect person with person, nation with nation, and event with event so that the influence of the gospel can increase exponentially. He simply needs a yielded heart that will pray the word and then invite the intervention of the Spirit as they pray.

Review Questions

4. What is intercession?
5. How does intercessory prayer differ from supplication?
6. Why do we need to pray for ministers?

Tweetable Moments

- An unhealthy appetite for conspiracy theories will inhibit your praying for the government. @MarcusTankard #PrayerSecrets
- You must meditate on the word more than you follow the issues if you want to be effective in praying for your nation. @MarcusTankard #Prayer Secrets
- You can exercise your authority over the social, economic and political arenas of your nation by speaking faith filled words. @MarcusTankard #PrayerSecrets

12 MINISTERS MANNA: IF YOU BUILD IT THEY WILL COME

I have a very special place in my heart for preachers. For years I believed this was because of my call to plant Bible schools. I have been actively working in Bible schools as a teacher and planter for the last six years. I feel right at home teaching, training, and sending ministers into the harvest. One encounter gave all of that a new meaning.

Our church hosted a minister out of Tulsa, Oklahoma for two services. This minister and her daughter ministered to my wife and I extensively during the course of those meetings. While we were in the minister's room, she went on to say some things to us that spoke directly to the stream of ministry in us. This began with her asking me about a direction for the service that night. I told her that we invited area ministers to be in attendance and wanted her to pray for our leaders and the visiting ministers if she felt led to do so.

I explained to her some of the things that I just stated about our heart for ministers. When I told her I thought this was because of our constant interaction with ministers in Bible schools, she corrected me prophetically. She said, "No, that's not why you love preachers. You love preachers because you are called to minister to them. God has called you that way and you will want to pay attention to how things take shape in this church and in your ministry in this area." I was stunned, but in my heart I knew it to be the truth.

Preachers, God has called you to be a world changer. As a minister, the most valuable tool that you have is God's Word in your mouth! This is why the devil fights you so hard. He doesn't want you to step into the office God has called you to and preach the Word of God!

When you preach the Word of God under the anointing, bondages break off of people, bodies are healed, people are saved, and whole regions are opened! All of this happens as a result of reaching your full potential in the office God has called you to. Miraculous things happen when you speak the Word with power and authority.

I want to help you get into the rooms and the phases of ministry that God has called you to. We thank God for people who pray for our ministries, but your prayer team does not negate your responsibility to pray out the plan of God for your own life. Sooner or later you are going to have to speak to the mountain for yourself. Your wife, mom, prayer team, or whoever prays for you can't do all the praying ALL the time. The just shall live by HIS OWN faith (Habakkuk 2:4; Hebrews 10:38).

Some of you who are reading this book have had prophecies spoken over you and you are twiddling your thumbs waiting on manifestation. Allow the truths in this book to jump-start your manifestation. Without faith it's impossible to please God (Hebrews 11:6). There are some simple truths in this book that will help to target your faith in this direction of manifestation.

What is faith? Faith is acting like the Word of God is true. Someone once said, "Faith is acting like God told you the truth." I have news for you: GOD TOLD YOU THE TRUTH! YOU ARE CALLED, ANOINTED, AND APPOINTED TO DO THE WORK OF GOD! God is not trying to embarrass you, and He won't let you embarrass Him.

You may be wondering, "Why would you title this chapter something so cliché as 'If You Build It They Will Come.'" These are the words that God spoke to me while I was praying for a minister. This particular minister and his wife were going through a transitional time in the ministry and God led me to pray for them. In this particular instance, God gave me a word for them. It began with the phrase, "If you build it, they will come."

God said, "If you'll build and construct the ministry you desire IN YOUR SPIRIT by speaking the Word and praying in the Holy Ghost, what is built in you will manifest through you!"

The Word Builds

Hebrews 11:3 NKJV
By faith we understand that the worlds were framed by the word of God, so that the things which are seen were not made of things which are visible.

Hebrews 11:3 AMP
By faith we understand that the worlds [during the successive ages] were framed (fashioned, put in order, and equipped for their intended purpose) by the word of God, so that what we see was not made out of things which are visible.

One of my instructors at Rhema once said, "The realm of the Spirit is more real than the realm of the natural." She went on to explain that the reason this is true, is because God (who is a Spirit, John 4:24) spoke words of faith from the spirit realm and those words went out of His mouth and created the world where we live today. This is possible because of the law of faith.

Romans 4:27 NKJV
Where is boasting then? It is excluded. By what law? Of works? No, but by the law of faith.

Faith is a law – or an established principle in the Word. But you must realize that just because it is written doesn't mean that it will go into motion automatically. You must get into the word and be well versed on how faith works so you can cooperate with the mechanics of the law. Then and only then will you get the benefit of it.

As ministers we have heard the

message on faith many times over. But just because you have heard the message doesn't necessarily mean you are DOING THE MESSAGE or receiving the BLESSING FROM THE MESSAGE. Romans 10:17 says, "Faith comes by hearing." But you must note that faith doesn't WORK BY HEARING. Let me say that again: Faith comes by hearing, but faith doesn't WORK by hearing.

If the law of faith is going to profit you, the mechanics of faith must be identified and put in motion. A great example of the law of faith in motion is Jesus and the fig tree.

Mark 11:12-14 NKJV
Now the next day, when they had come out from Bethany, He was hungry. And seeing from afar a fig tree having leaves, He went to see if perhaps He would find something on it. When He came to it, He found nothing but leaves, for it was not the season for figs. In response Jesus said to it, "Let no one eat fruit from you ever again." And His disciples heard it.

Mark 11:20-24
Now in the morning, as they passed by, they saw the fig tree dried up from the roots. And Peter, remembering, said to Him, "Rabbi, look! The fig tree which You cursed has withered away." So Jesus answered and said to them, "Have faith in God. For assuredly, I say to you, whoever says to this mountain, 'Be removed and be cast into the sea,' and does not doubt in his heart, but believes that those things he says will be done, he will have whatever he says. Therefore I say to you, whatever things you ask when you pray, believe that you receive them, and you will have them.

Jesus spoke to the fig tree and the next day he and the disciples walked by the same tree that He spoke to the day before and saw it had dried up from the root. There's a message right here on faith that could change your life if you will let it. When you begin to speak the word over your situation, it may seem like nothing happens – in fact things may get a little worse. But don't worry about it! The scripture says that the tree dried up from the root. Trees dry up from the outside – not from the root. This is a beautiful picture of how faith works. When the Word is spoken out of your mouth it goes straight to the root of the situation.

So Jesus proceeds to give the disciples a lesson on the law of faith. He says, "WHOSOEVER shall SAY..." This is the first and most important element to the law of faith: SPEAKING! Jesus said, "Whosoever shall say unto this mountain be removed and be cast into the sea and will not doubt in his heart, but will believe that those things which he says will come to pass, he will have what he says." Faith comes by hearing, but it WORKS BY SPEAKING!

Notice that Jesus said, "Whosoever shall say..." So that tells me that you've got to say something. As a minister, you are going to have to SAY something about your ministry. What are you SAYING? It doesn't matter how many books you READ ABOUT THE MINISTRY or how many MINISTERS CONFERENCES you attend or how many MINISTRY CONSULTANTS you meet with – if you don't SAY about your ministry, you will never see the manifestation of your vision.

You can have journals and notebooks of prophecies concerning what God has spoken to your heart and through others about your ministry, but if you don't have anything to SAY about your ministry, your ministry will not grow. You must realize that you won't have what God says about your ministry; you will only have what YOU say about your ministry. So I'll ask you again, "What are you saying about your ministry?"

Lets Build!

The book of Hebrews says that it was faith that caused the earth to be formed, fashioned, put in order, and equipped for its intended purpose. In other words, the world was BUILT by the spoken word of God. God spoke and saw what He said (Genesis 1). God is telling you that if you want a powerful ministry, you are going to have to build it with your words! YOU build it. Not God. YOU.

God has done His part: He called you, anointed you, and gave you a vision. Now you need to take what He gave you and build. Not go out and try to make something happen. NO! Use God's Word in your mouth to build God's vision of ministry for you. If God said it, then His words are equipped with His ability to do what He said.

John 1:1 NKJV
In the beginning was the Word, and the Word was with God, and the Word was God.

Hebrews 4:12 NKJV
the word of God is living and powerful, and sharper than any two-edged sword, piercing even to the division of soul and spirit, and of joints and marrow, and is a discerner of the thoughts and intents of the heart.

God and His word are one. You can't separate the two. In fact He said that He exalted His Word above His name (Psalms 138:2). His Word is alive because it is the very substance of His Person. So when you release the Word of God over your ministry, you are releasing the creative ability of God to frame, fashion, put things in order and equip your future for His intended purpose for your life.

When God spoke and built the world in Genesis, His words went out into infinite darkness. The world was an abyss that was void of light and life. If God had of been one of us, would He have waited for someone else to come and prophesy over the condition of the earth or called a church consultant to diagnose the problem and give constructive criticism?

No, God grabbed the creative power within Himself, infused His words with that power, sent those words out to perform His purpose, and today we are experiencing the benefits of that work of art that began with His words in Genesis.

God has not changed! What would happen if you took His Word and put it on your ministry? How many people could be saved if you dared to speak God's words over your ministry? How many members could your church have if you would speak God's words over your church? How effective could your staff be if you spoke God's words over them daily?

Preachers are looking for gimmicks and quick growth schemes and marketing strategies. God's not going to build ministries like that. He will build ministries the same way that He built the world - FAITH FILLED WORDS. It begins by you hearing what thus saith the Lord concerning your ministry. His words to your heart are the building materials that you use to build a ministry for Him and to His glory. How do you build? With your mouth. Jeremiah called the word of God a hammer (Jeremiah 23:29). Put that hammer to work by speaking it and watch how it takes NOTHING and turns it into SOMETHING.

Don't Wait, SPEAK!

Years ago I was at a very important crossroads in my ministry. I could either take one path, which was very predictable and comfortable, or I could step out on nothing and pursue my dream: the call of God to do missions. I didn't know what to do. While I wanted to do missions work, I didn't even know where to start. Everything down this particular road looked void, dark and without form (Genesis 1:1,2).

I was having dinner with a ministry couple in Tulsa and I endeavored to explain my dilemma to them. They listened to me so patiently. Once I got everything out of my system, the wife spoke up and said, "Why don't you build the perfect position in ministry with your words?" What she said took me by surprise. She said, "Decide what you want out of the next ministry position/adventure, then speak it out of your mouth. Watch your heart to see if it agrees."

She went on to say, "If don't sense your heart agreeing with what your mouth is saying, stop. Seek the Lord some more. Pray in the Spirit for a few days and draw out the wisdom of God. Then speak out what you believe He's saying. There are times when you have to confess things out of your mouth to see how your heart will witness with it. If there is a witness there, it's because the Spirit of truth is guiding you. Keep speaking it and allow it to CREATE A ROOM FOR YOU IN THE SPIRIT."

This proved to be a priceless gem for me in the ministry. I took what she shared with me and I did it. At the time I wanted to work for a local church as a prayer leader and have the liberty to travel. I knew that it was an unusual position, but that's what burned on my heart

When I left my job in Tulsa, I moved to Alabama. A friend of mine had pioneered a work in Dothan. I attended the church a few times and decided to join. It just so happened that the pastor wanted to develop their prayer department. So I got busy! As I served in that church as a pray-er and as a singer on their worship team, the pastor recognized the gift of God in me and helped to launch me into the mission field.

While I was in Tulsa, I had pages and pages of things the Lord had shared with me about going to the mission field. The church that I attended in Tulsa hosted guest ministers regularly. Many of them prophesied to me concerning my calling. But I never stepped into it or even made steps toward it until I began to BUILD MY FUTURE with my own WORDS.

I pray that you are getting what I'm saying here. Your ministry begins by faith, is kept by faith, and it is progressed by faith! Jesus is the Author and the Finisher of your faith. He will finish what He authored in you, but He will do it by way of YOUR MOUTH! You must speak! As you speak, the Word will go out and produce the dream God placed in your heart.

Praying in the Holy Ghost Builds

Jude 20 NKJV
But you, beloved, building yourselves up on your most holy faith, praying in the Holy Spirit...

This scripture has a revelation in plain view that we have been teaching around for years. It plainly states, BUILDING yourself up... PRAYING IN THE HOLY SPIRIT. Some ministers, myself included, have taught this scripture and said this is simply edifying yourself. Paul said that when you speak in an unknown tongue, you edify yourself (1Corinthians 14:2-4), so this idea is a biblical one. But this is not an all-inclusive expose' of this scripture by no means.

Build yourself up. The Amplified version says, "Rise higher and higher like an edifice." I like to say, rise from one degree of anointing to another. Did you know that as a minister there are measures to the anointing? The anointing can increase on your life and ministry. Why is this important? The anointing determines the influence and the fruit that accompanies your ministry (Isaiah 10:27).

How do you increase the anointing on your ministry? Kenneth E. Hagin said in his book Understanding the Anointing that you can increase the anointing by praying and fasting. As you pray and fast, your spirit becomes more sensitive to God and the leading of the Spirit. In fact, you become more conscious of the leading of the Spirit and you are less likely to miss His promptings when you are aware of Him in this way.

However, I want to delve into this reality a little deeper. There are many things that take place when you pray in other tongues. You can pray for the unknown (Romans 8:26), magnify God

(1 Acts 10:44- 46), edify yourself (1 Corinthians 14:2-4), and refresh yourself (Isaiah 28:12). But I want to examine this in more detail because in it we will find Holy Spirit cooperating with us as we build.

The Holy Spirit the Revealer of Secrets

1 Corinthians 2:9-10 NKJV
But as it is written: "Eye has not seen, nor ear heard, Nor have entered into the heart of man the things which God has prepared for those who love Him." But God has revealed them to us through His Spirit. For the Spirit searches all things, yes, the deep things of God.

1 Corinthians 2:10 AMP
Yet to us God has unveiled and revealed them by and through His Spirit, for the [Holy] Spirit searches diligently, exploring and examining everything, even sounding the profound and bottomless things of God [the divine counsels and things hidden and beyond man's scrutiny].

Notice that this says what is hidden from your eyes, ears, and heart has now been revealed by the ministry of the Holy Spirit. The Holy Spirit is the Revealer of secrets. "What secrets," you may ask. It may be a mystery to your understanding, but the Holy Spirit knows everything about everybody all the time – including God's plan for your life.
Jesus said that the Holy Spirit would take of what He has and give it to you freely.

All the Father has belongs to Jesus, so the Holy Spirit is receiving intelligence from God the Father and Jesus Christ about you. Isn't that interesting? Everything that God has to say about the anointing on your life and how that anointing is supposed to operate, has been given to the Holy Spirit.

Acts 19:11-12 NKJV
Now God worked unusual miracles by the hands of Paul, so that even handkerchiefs or aprons were brought from his body to the sick, and the diseases left them and the evil spirits went out of them.

God worked unusual miracles through Paul. Or we could say it this way: Paul had an anointing for unusual miracles. Ed Dufresne references this scripture with Hebrews 2:4 when he teaches on specialty anointings. What does that mean? As a minister, you are set in the body of Christ as it pleases Him (1 Corinthians 12:18). God will anoint you and equip you with special anointings that will accommodate and enhance your calling.

God hasn't changed. He's still anointing people with specialty anointings today. Paul encouraged us to covet spiritual gifts and to excel in them. Many of us are hungry for the move of the Spirit in this manner, but are at a lost of words as to how to "move into this flow." Our eyes haven't seen this, ears haven't heard, and our hearts don't completely understand what we are longing for. It's the gifts of the Spirit on a higher order than what we have experienced before.

Many of you reading this book have had dreams and visions of yourself flowing in the supernatural. God has been speaking to some of you about the healing ministry. In addition to seeing some things in the Spirit and hearing God speak to your heart, people may have prophesied to you. These operations of the Spirit are so real to you, it's like you can almost touch them.

What's the solution? Wait on God to just initiate something on His own? Just kind of twiddle our thumbs and just hope that if we sing enough songs or preach the right sermon, something will just pop out and we'll miraculously find ourselves overflowing in manifestation? Nope...that's not the way to do it. God gave us help by sending the person of the Holy Ghost.

The Holy Ghost will bring these manifestations to us. The Amplified version says that the Holy Spirit will search diligently, exploring and examining everything. What does that mean? It means that the Spirit of God will search the mind of God concerning His will and plan for your life. He will search out the expression and flow of power that God has intended to flow through you. He will search the purpose for which He placed you in the Body.

Then it says that He will SOUND these BOTTOMLESS TRUTHS to your SPIRIT. I like to say He will VOICE AND ANNOUNCE these things to our spirits. 1 Corinthians 14:2-4 says that when a man prays in an unknown tongue He speaks mysteries. What are mysteries? The mysteries are the hidden secrets. And it is in that speaking that you BUILD YOURSELF! You build your MINISTRY. You build EXPRESSION OF GIFTINGS. You build MANIFESTATIONS. And as you build, an awareness of who God has made you to be comes to your heart (Ephesians 2:10). A greater revelation of His workmanship in you and the equipment He's given you comes to your heart as you speak and pray.

Romans 8:26-27 Likewise the Spirit also helps in our weaknesses. For we do not know what we should pray for as we ought, but the Spirit Himself makes intercession for us with groanings which cannot be uttered. Now He who searches the hearts knows what the mind of the Spirit is, because He makes intercession for the saints according to the will of God.

As you are praying in the Holy Spirit, this river of prayer is flowing through your heart. The flow has a dual working: it is cleansing your heart of the impure motives and carnal plans of man and depositing thoughts from the mind and will of God. You may say, "How is this possible?" It's really simple when you consider that the language of the Spirit is the plan of God. The Spirit of God is going to inspire you to pray what has been revealed to Him from the Father concerning His plan for your life.

As you pray in the Spirit, you are praying God's perfect will for your life.

His plan is being imparted to your spirit. Prayer is the first place you encounter God's unique calling for your life (Jeremiah 29:11- 12).

Praying in the Holy Spirit is designed to equip you from the inside out. It affects the part of you where all permanent change comes – your spirit.

Many places in the Bible where it uses the term heart, it is referring to the human spirit. Proverbs says to guard your heart with all diligence for out it flows the issues of life (Proverbs 4:23). Or I like to say it this way: for out of it comes the issuing of life.

Your heart is designed to bring life to whatever is planted there. This is why you want to continuously plant the Word in your heart. God has set this thing up in such a way that your heart will nourish your entire life. But you have to plant the proper seeds. What are the proper seeds? The Word of God and the mysteries of God.

Are you in need of peace? Plant peace seeds. Are you in need of money? Plant money seeds. Are you in need of love? Plant love seeds. Are you in need of faith? Plant faith seeds. Are you in need of healing? Plant healing seeds. Do you desire your ministry to grow, increase, and expand? Plant ministry seeds.

Grab the Word of God and dare to speak and declare it over your calling. Then don't stop there. PRAY IN THE HOLY GHOST. As you do that, you are pulling on the powers of the age. You are pulling the infinite wisdom of the Spirit. According to Romans, you are studying the mind of a Genius and giving voice to His thoughts in an unknown tongue.

What is all this doing? It is building the gifts and the operations of the Spirit in your heart. If you build it, they will come. What will come? Whatever it is that you've been praying for, confessing about, and believing for. Are you in need of opportunities? If you build it, they will come. Do you desire a greater flow of the gifts of the Spirit through you and your ministry? If you build it, they will come. Do you want to increase the influence of your ministry in the community? If you build it, they will come!

How do you build? Speaking the word and praying in the Holy Ghost. Notice that Jude 20 says, "Building up yourselves..." It didn't say, "Let God build you up." No, it said, "building up yourselves." God has given you the building materials of the Word and the Spirit. God has a plan for your life, but you must pray it out with the tools that He has already given you.

You have the tools at your disposal. Don't wait any longer. You may say, "Well Pastor Marcus I don't know where to start. I know I'm called to preach, but I don't know what I'm supposed to be doing. I don't even know what ministry gift I'm supposed to be in." Well start confessing what you do know. Say this out loud:

I'm called, appointed and anointed to preach the gospel. In the name of Jesus I cast out demons and lay hands on the sick. The gifts of the Spirit are available to me and I will reach my full potential in the office or offices that God has called me to. There is coming full disclosure of the plan of God to me. I am His workmanship created in Christ unto good works. Those works are no longer a mystery to me in Jesus' name.

Then pray in the Holy Ghost. As you pray, watch to see what He will say to you. See, it's when you get into the flow of this, that the gifts of the Spirit will begin operating in your prayer time. Kenneth Hagin called it the spirit of seeing and knowing. Your eyes will be opened to see what you didn't see before. Your ears will be open to hear what you haven't heard before. Your heart will begin to discern and comprehend the plan of God more clearly.

As God reveals these things to you, write them down. Study them. Meditate on them. Search the scriptures concerning them. Faith comes by hearing the Word (Romans 1:17). So search the Word for further revelation on what God is saying to you.

Dare to speak out of your mouth what was spoken to you. This all goes back to believing and speaking. Speak what God said to you in prayer throughout the day. Then pray in the Holy Ghost some more. What are you doing? You are praying out God's plan. If you will pray it out, you can walk it out.

The ball is in your court. Start building. Some of you need to read this chapter a couple more times and allow these truths to really sink into your spirit.

These are simple truths, but they are powerful and monumental to those who will do what has been written.

Review Questions

1. How does the law of faith work in the life of a minister?
2. How can ministers cooperate with God and build a ministry?
3. How does the Holy Spirit reveal God's plan to us for ministry?

Tweetable Moments

- The realm of the spirit is more real than the realm of the natural. @MarcusTankard #PrayerSecrets
- God will anoint you and equip you with special anointings that will accommodate and enhance your calling. @MarcusTankard #PrayerSecrets
- As you pray in the Spirit, watch to see what He will say to you. @MarcusTankard #PrayerSecrets

MEDITATION MANUAL

Jeremiah 33:3 Call to Me, and I will answer you and show you great and mighty things, which you do not know.
(TLB) Ask me and I will tell you some remarkable secrets about what is going to happen here.
(AMP) Call to Me, and I will answer you and show you great and mighty things, fenced in and hidden, which you do not know (do not distinguish and recognize, have knowledge of and understand).

Matthew 7:7 Ask, and it will be given to you; seek, and you will find knock, and it will be opened to you.
(Johnson) Here are three simple directives for living in the Spirit dimension…
(K. & L.) …knock, and you will gain admission.

Matthew 7:8 For everyone who asks receives, and he who seeks finds, and to him who knocks it will be opened.

(Mof) …for everyone who asks receives, the seeker finds, the door is open to anyone who knocks.

Mark 11:24 Therefore I say to you, whatever things you ask when you pray, believe that you receive them, and you will have them.
(Johnson) Because of this principle, when you discover your soul's deepest desires, state them in your prayers, and consider them to have occurred – they will!
(Mof.) …believe you have got it and you shall have it.

John 15:7 If you abide in Me, and My words abide in you, you will ask what you desire, and it shall be done for you.
(Wuest) If you maintain a living communion with me and my words are at home in you, I command you to ask, at once, something for yourself, whatever your heart desires, and it will become yours.
(K. & L.) As long as you remain united with me, and my teachings remain your rule of life, you may ask for anything you wish, and you shall have it.

John 16:23 And in that day you will ask Me nothing. Most assuredly, I say to you,

whatever you ask the Father in My name He will give you.
(TLB) At that time you won't need to ask me for anything, for you can go directly to the Father and ask him, and he will give you what you ask for because you use my name.
(Knox) …Believe me, you have only to make any request of the Father in my life, and he will grant it to you.

Acts 4:24 So when they heard that, they raised their voice to God with one accord and said: "Lord, You are God, who made heaven and earth and the sea, and all that is in them."
(Rieu) …they raised their voices to God in unity of spirit…
(NEB) …they raised their voices as one man and called upon God…
(Trans.) …they all prayed out loud to God together…

Acts 4:29 Now, Lord, look on their threats, and grant to Your servants that with all boldness they may speak Your word.
(Roth. 2) …give to thy servants with all freedom of utterance to be speaking thy word…
(Phil.) …give they servants courage to speak thy word fearlessly…
(AMP) …grant to Your bond servants [full freedom] to declare Your message fearlessly…

Acts 4:30 By stretching out Your hand to heal, and that signs and wonders may be done through the name of Your holy Servant Jesus.
(Barclay) …and act yourself to heal and to cause wonderful demonstrations of your power to happen through the name of your holy servant Jesus.
(Wade) …by exerting They Active Power to bring about Healing

Romans 8:26 Likewise the Spirit also helps in our weaknesses. For we do not know what we should pray for as we ought, but the Spirit Himself makes intercession for us with groanings which cannot be uttered.
(Wuest) …the Spirit lends us a helping hand with reference to our weakness, for the particular thing we should pray for according to what is necessary in the nature of the case, we do not know with an absolute knowledge.
(Phil.) …helps us in our present limitations…
(Black.) …the Spirit gives assistance in our weakness – he takes hold [of our problems] on the other side…

Romans 8:27 Now He who searches the hearts knows what the mind of the Spirit is, because He makes intercession for the saints according to the will of God.
(Jordan) …he who X-rays our hearts…
(Weym.) …His intercessions for God's people are in harmony with God's will.

1 Corinthians 14:2 For he who speaks in a tongue does not speak to men but to God, for no one understands him; however, in the spirit he speaks mysteries.
(Mof.) …he is talking of divine secrets in the Spirit.
(Authentic) …He is speaking mysterious things in spirit language.
(Weym.) …In the Spirit he is speaking secret truths.

1 Corinthians 14:4 He who speaks in a tongue edifies himself, but he who prophesies edifies the church.
(AMP) …edifies and improves himself…
(NAB) …builds up himself

1 Corinthians 14:14 For if I pray in a tongue, my spirit prays, but my understanding is unfruitful.
(GNB) …my spirit prays indeed, but my mind has no part in it.
(NEB) …my intellect lies fallow.
(NAB) …my spirit is at prayer but my mind contributes nothing.
(AMP) My spirit (by the Holy Spirit within me) prays, but my mind is unproductive…
(Wuest) …my spirit [the human spirit as moved by the Holy Spirit] is praying.

1 Corinthians 14:15 What is the conclusion then I will pray with the spirit, and I will also pray with the understanding. I will sing with the spirit, and I will also sing with the understanding.
(AMP) …I will pray with my spirit [by the Holy Spirit that is within me]…I will sing with my spirit [by the Holy Spirit that is within me]…
(Wuest) I will pray by means of my spirit. But I will pray also with the aid of my intellect.

Ephesians 6:18 Praying always with all prayer and supplication in the Spirit, being watchful to this end with all perseverance and supplication for all the saints…
(AMP) Pray at all times (on every occasion, in every season) in the Spirit, with all (manner of) prayer and entreaty. To that end keep alert and watch with strong purpose and perseverance, interceding in behalf of all the saints (God's consecrated people).
(Johnson) Cultivate a continuous attitude of payer both for yourself and for the family of God.
(Gspd.) Use every kind of prayer and entreaty, and at every opportunity pray in the Spirit. Be on the alert about it; devote yourselves constantly to prayer.
(Wms.) Keep on praying in the Spirit, with every kind of prayer and entreaty, at every opportunity…
(Beck) Pray at all times in the Spirit, using every kind of prayer. Be alert and keep at it

continually…

Philippians 4:6 Be anxious for nothing, but in everything by prayer and supplication, with thanksgiving, let your requests be made known to God;
(RSV, Gspd.) Have no anxiety about anything…
(Letters) Don't worry about anything but talk to the Father about everything. Tell him what you need and keep thanking Him.
(Knox) Nothing must make you anxious; in every need make your requests known to God…
(Jer.) There is no need to worry; but if there is anything you need, pray for it, asking God for it with prayer and thanksgiving.
(NAB) Dismiss all anxiety from your minds. Present your needs to God in every form of prayer and in petitions full of gratitude.

1 John 5:14 Now this is the confidence that we have in Him, that if we ask anything according to His will, he hears us.
(Barclay) The reason why we can approach God with complete confidence is that, if we ask for anything that is in accordance with His will, he listens to us.
(Knox) Such familiar confidence we have in him…
(Roth. 2) And this is the freedom of speech which we have towards him…
(GNB) We have courage in God's presence, because we are sure that he hears us if we ask him for anything that is according to his will.

1 John 5:15 And if we known that He hears u, whatever we ask, we know that we have the petitions that we have asked of Him.

Jude 20 But you, beloved, building yourselves up on your most holy faith, praying in the Holy Spirit…
(AMP) But you, beloved, build yourselves up [founded] on your most holy faith [make progress, rise like an edifice higher and higher] praying in the Holy Spirit
(Jer.) But you, my dear friends, must use your most holy faith as your foundation and build on that, praying in the Holy Spirit…
(NEB) …fortify yourselves in your most sacred faith…

Scriptures are New King James Version unless otherwise marked.
Translations used in the text are identified by the abbreviations as noted below.

AMP *Amplified Bible.* Zondervan Publishing House, Grand Rapids, Michigan, 1972

Barclay Barclay, William. *The New Testament, A New Translation.* Collins, London, England, 1968

Beck Beck, William. *The Holy Bible in the Language of Today.* A.J. Hollman Company, New York, New York, 1976.

Black. Blackwelder, Boyce. *Letters from Paul, An Exegetical Translation.* Warner Press, Anderson, Indiana, 1971

GNB *Good News Bible, The Bible in Today's English Version.* American Bible Society, New York, New York, 1976

Gspd. Goodspeed, Edgar J. *The New Testament, An American Translation.* University of Chicago, Chicago, Illinois, 1923

Johnson Johnson, Ben Campbell. *Matthew and Mark, A Rational Paraphrase of the New Testament.* Word Books, Waco, Texas, 1987

Johnson Johnson, Ben Campbell. *The Heart of Paul, A Rational Paraphrase of the New Testament.* Word Books, Waco, Texas, 1976

Jordan Jordan , Clarence. *The Cotton Patch Version of Paul's Epistles.* Association Press, New York, New York, 1968.

K. & L. Kleist, James A and Lilly, Joseph L. *The New Testament Rendered from the Original Greek with Explanatory Notes.* The Bruce Publishing Company, Milqaukee, Wisconsin, 1956

Knox Knox, Ronald. *The New Testament of Our Lord and Savior Jesus Christ, A New Translation.* Sheed and Ward, New York, New York, 1953

Letters *Letters to Street Christians by Two Brothers from Berkeley.* Zondervan Publishing House, Grand Rapids, Michigan, 1971

Mof. Moffat, James. *The Holy Bible Containing the Old and New Testaments.* Double Day and Company, Inc., New York, New York, 1926.

NAB *New American Bible.* Thomas Nelson Publishers, New York, New York, 1975

NEB *New English Bible.* Oxford University Press, Oxford, England, 1961

Phil. Phillips, J.B. *The New testament in Modern English* The Macmillan Company, New York, New York, 1958

Ricu Rieu, E.V. *The Acts of the Apostles.* The Penguin Books, London, England, 1957

Roth. 2 Rotherham, J.B. *The New Testament: Critically Emphasized.* John Wiley and Sons, New York, New York, 1896

RSV *Revised Standard Version.* Thomas Nelson and Sons, New York, New York, 1952

TLB Taylor, Ken. *The Living Bible.* Tyndale House Publishers, Wheaton, Illinois, 1971

Trans. *The Translator's New Testament.* The Fleming H. Revell Company, New York, New York, 1902

Wade Wade, G.W. *The Documents of the New Testament.* Thomas Burby and Company, London, England, 1934

Weym. Weymouth, Richard Francis. *The New Testament.* James Clark and Company, London, England, 1909

Wms. Williams, Charles G. *The New Testament.* Moody Press, Chicago, Illinois, 1978

Wuest Wuest, Kenneth S. *The New Testament, An Expanded translation.* William B. Eerdmans Publishing Company, Grand Rapids, Michigan, 1981

ABOUT THE AUTHOR

Marcus Tankard – star of the hit Bravo TV reality series "Thicker Than Water" – is a missionary, pastor, musician and author. Marcus has spent over fifteen years preaching and teaching the Word of God in Bible schools, churches, on television and on radio. He received Bible training from Rhema Bible Training Center in Tulsa, Oklahoma. After graduating from Bible school, Marcus founded and planted two Bible schools in the Czech Republic – Apostolos Bible Training Center. For more information, visit www.marcustankard.com.

Made in the USA
Middletown, DE
18 July 2021